Are You a Conservative or a Liberal?

Other Works by Victor Kamber

Giving Up on Democracy:
Why Term Limits Are Bad for America

Other Works By Bradley O'Leary

Presidential Follies: Those Who Would
Be President and Those Who Should Think Again
(with Ralph Hallow)

Top 200 Reasons <u>Not</u> to Vote for Bill Clinton

Dining by Candlelight:
America's 200 Most Romantic Restaurants *

Bed & Champagne:
Top Romantic Hideaways *

* *forthcoming from Boru Publishing*

ARE YOU A

Conservative

➡

OR A

Liberal?

⬅

A Fun and Easy Test to
Tell Where You Stand on
the Political Spectrum

Victor Kamber and
Bradley O'Leary

Library of Congress Catalog Card Number: 96-85050

ISBN 1-887161-09-0 (pbk)
ISBN 1-887161-19-8

Published in the United States by
Boru Publishing, Inc.
12004-B Commonwealth Way
Austin, TX 78759

Distributed to the trade by
National Book Network, Inc.
4720 Boston Way
Lanham, MD 20706

Boru books are available in quantity for promotional or premium use. For information on discounts and terms, please write to Director of Special Sales, Boru Publishing, Inc., 12004-B Commonwealth Way, Austin, Texas 78759.

Cover design by Tom Tafuri
Manufactured in the United States of America

5 4 3 2 1

This book is dedicated to Senator John Tower (R-TX), who honed my beliefs and thoughts, gave me a political direction, and was my mentor and friend. Also, to his daughter, Jeanne Tower Cox, who has made sure that his accomplishments and service to America will be remembered as long as this country exists.

This book is also dedicated to Duncan Bauman, former publisher of the *St. Louis Globe Democrat*, who started me on the road to conservative beliefs.

— Bradley S. O'Leary

Acknowledgments

Thanks to Craig Shirley of Craig Shirley & Associates for helping us develop the questions and answers for our political tests. And thanks to Stephen Weeks, whose brilliant editorial skills made this book a truly bipartisan endeavor.

Contents

1 / Which Side Are You On?

Are you a liberal or a conservative? Do you know where you stand on the issues? Are you sure?

This book is designed to help you answer these questions and to provoke further questions and a lively debate. Americans are lucky to live in a democracy. Democracy is the most fair and responsive form of government. It's also the most fun. A great deal of life is taken up with political debate. Whether you're a political professional, an activist, or just an interested voter, the American political system is a source of endless fascination because everything is up for discussion—and sometimes the firing line can get pretty hot.

Political battles in our country are fought by the warring camps of liberals and conservatives. That's not just an arbitrary distinction created by newspaper editors and television producers seeking to stir up easy controversies. In fact, it makes a lot of sense. Liberalism and conservatism are two opposing value systems that go to the core of human nature. The conflict between these two ideologies has animated politics from the beginning.

Throughout history, in almost every circumstance in which citizens were allowed to participate in their own government, two sides quickly rose: the newly emerging classes against those with vested interests, progress against reaction. The terms "left" and "right" were coined during the French Assembly, where the more conservative members sat on the right and the liberal faction sat on the left. Similar divisions can be seen in political systems everywhere, particularly in the world's longest running democracy—the United States.

For most of American history, there have been two political parties. First there were Jefferson's Democrats and Hamilton's Federalists. Then the Whigs rose and fell. Just before the Civil War, a new party emerged: the Republicans. Now there are noises from frustrated citizens from the left, right, and center to create a new party. But the only way a third party has ever succeeded in America was by replacing a major party that no longer speaks for its natural constituency. The parties that survive represent not just opposing interests, but different ideologies, which can basically be characterized as liberal and conservative.

But what is a liberal? What is a conservative? When people use these terms, what do they mean?

To oversimplify the issue enormously, let's say that your personal political position is based on how you feel about the government. Liberals believe that government can be a positive force in people's lives; they try to use political power to make needed changes in the economy and society. Conservatives believe that government should be limited; they try to use it only to defend the country from either internal or external threats.

Whether you're a liberal or a conservative has a lot to do with how you view human nature. Liberal philosophers like Jean Jacques Rousseau believed that people were naturally good and only corrupted by the evil world. Therefore, a government that protected and developed that natural goodness was necessary. Conservative philosophers like Thomas Hobbes believed that human nature was to be subdued by evil and that government should be used to protect people from each other.

Let's translate these abstract philosophical disagreements into the concrete realities of an issue such as crime. Liberals seek to control criminals not only through punishment but by attacking the root causes of crime—poverty and neglect. They believe that, if more people have an honest chance in society, then they won't turn to crime. Conservatives see crime as a moral issue. Forget about whether the criminals were deprived or abused—conservatives feel criminals ought to pay for their transgressions against society and they believe that evil people do exist and there is no redemption in this life for them.

You could say that liberals are optimistic, and conservatives are pessimists. Or you could say that liberals are irresponsible idealists, and conservatives are sober realists. It all depends on which side you're on.

So which side are you on? How do you feel about your government? Do you think it takes too much out of your paycheck, or do you get worthwhile security and services in return? When you see the U.S. Capitol on television, does it make you want a Congress that works every day or one that just meets six months a year? Does it make you think of the great legislative achievements of the federal government—such as work place safety standards and the Civil Rights Act—or are you reminded of the restrictions on your business and your right to own a gun? What do you think of President Bill Clinton? Is he a noninhaling, dope-smoking, draft-dodging liar? Or is he a good man trying to do an impossible job? What do you think of his wife Hillary Rodham Clinton? Is she a brilliant career woman or some Lady Macbeth on the make? How about Speaker Newt Gingrich? Is he a visionary or a buffoon? A revolutionary who shakes things up in Washington or a crass politician who shakes funders down? Do you agree with his political agenda? Would you like to have him over for dinner?

Opinions are like belly buttons—everybody has them. But political opinions are more than just matters of taste or habit. They are some of the most important judgments citizens make. After all, when people express their opinions in the voting booth, they both elect their leaders and determine how their country is going to be run. That's why it's important to know where you stand.

Liberals and conservatives each pursue clearly different political agendas. Liberals believe that many rules should be set from Washington, DC. Conservatives believe that the rules should be set by local government at the lowest possible level. Again, to enormously oversimplify things, conservatives want less government interference in the economy and more government intervention in citizens' private lives. Liberals want greater government intervention in the economy and less interference in citizens' private lives. As *Washington Post* columnist E. J. Dionne describes it, liberals want the government to put its hand in their pockets, but keep it out of their pants. Conservatives want the government's hand out of their pockets and in their pants.

Of course, there are always exceptions. Not every conservative believes 100 percent in the right-wing agenda. And not every liberal follows the party line. Sometimes the issues themselves defy easy categorization. For example, in the 1996 Republican primaries, Pat Buchanan—who is somewhere to the right of most candidates—came out in favor of tariffs and trade barriers. Protectionist trade policy used to be a conservative issue in the late nineteenth and early twentieth centuries. But as business interests became more global (or, as they said back then, international), conservatives gradually turned more toward the free market. Then it was the liberals who increasingly called for tariffs to protect the jobs and wages of American workers. Now many liberals and most conservatives advocate "free trade," whereas others from both groups argue for "fair trade."

Free speech issues also defy easy categorization. Many conservatives are libertarians. They believe that the government belongs neither in our pockets nor in our pants. Libertarian conservatives insist on a limited government providing only for national defense, the court system, and police protection. Everything else—like schools, roads, lighthouses, parklands, and the poor—should be taken care of by the private sector. They believe in absolute free speech, even if they consider it immoral (e.g., pornography) or unpatriotic (e.g., burning the flag). Other conservatives believe there is a limit to First Amendment rights. They want to regulate or ban pornography and make flag burning unconstitutional. The battle between libertarian and traditionalist conservatives is personified in the fight between Phil Gramm and Pat Buchanan. They are diametrically opposed on trade issues, yet they both call themselves conservatives.

Liberals find themselves in a similar schism when it comes to the issue of national defense. Many liberals became politically involved during the Vietnam War, and antiwar activism is their most deeply felt political belief. These liberals are usually against foreign intervention. However, more traditional liberals, who are philosophically closer to Hubert Humphrey than his fellow Minnesota liberal Eugene McCarthy, want to use American military strength to establish and protect democracy around the world. These liberals often favor foreign intervention.

Despite the fact that these categories aren't always perfect, the terms "liberal" and "conservative" do provide general guidelines to determining your political beliefs. However, even though you might hear the terms liberal and conservative daily in the media and you might follow politics with active interest, perhaps you're not exactly sure which side you're on yourself. That's why we have created a test to measure your opinions on the issues and give you a fairly accurate idea of where you stand. You might already know whether you're a liberal or a conservative. Or you might think you're comfortably in the middle of the road. Even if you're pretty certain about your political position, you still might be surprised to see how you score.

Are you a fire-breathing right-winger or a bomb-throwing lefty? Are you a rock-ribbed Republican or a yellow-dog Democrat? Do you believe in God and country or the separation of church and state? Are you a liberal or a conservative?

Take our test and find out.

2 / The Quiz

Here is our brand new political quiz. Take it and you'll be able to find out where you stand on the political spectrum. Record your responses and then compare them with the answer section at the end of this chapter. Unless noted otherwise circle only one response to each question.

If you find some of these questions challenging, congratulations! They are supposed to be tough enough to force you to think carefully and then make a decision.

1. Which of the following would you prefer?
   a) An activist government that can provide more services even if it means higher taxes
   b) A smaller, less activist government that provides fewer services, which means lower taxes

2. Which national legislation would you support? (Circle all that apply.)
   a) Allow voluntary prayer in school
   b) Ban the sale of handguns other than to the military and police
   c) Ban flag burning
   d) Enact term limits for U.S. legislators

3. If each of these authors had a new novel in the stores, whose would you read?
   a) Tom Clancy
   b) John Grisham

4. Which TV show would you watch?
   a) *Walker, Texas Ranger*
   b) *Friends*

5. **Which Supreme Court justice has views more aligned with yours?**
   a) Clarence Thomas
   b) Ruth Ginsberg

6. **Would you prefer a flat tax, in which all income is taxed at the same rate and tax forms are simpler, or a graduated tax, in which higher incomes are taxed at a higher rate and lower incomes at a lower rate?**
   a) Flat tax
   b) Graduated tax

7. **Should companies be encouraged through government policies, such as tax breaks, to lay off fewer workers, even if it means lower corporate tax revenues?**
   a) Yes
   b) No

8. **If you saw a child watching a wedding between two homosexual individuals on television, would you change the channel?**
   a) Yes
   b) No

9. **What should be the primary goal of America's foreign policy?**
   a) To promote democracy and human rights around the world
   b) To serve U.S. national interests

10. **Do you object to religious displays, such as nativity scenes at Christmas or menorahs at Hanukkah, on government property?**
    a) Yes
    b) No

11. **Who should have the greater voice in deciding what books children read in school?**
    a) Parents
    b) Teachers

12. **Should tests for the human immunodeficiency virus (HIV), the virus that causes acquired immunodeficiency syndrome (AIDS), be mandatory for professional athletes in contact sports (e.g., boxing, football, wrestling)?**
    a) Yes
    b) No

13. **Do you support a voucher system that would allow parents to send their children to the public or private school of their choice?**
    a) Yes
    b) No

14. **With whom would you prefer to have lunch?**
    a) Paul Newman
    b) Charlton Heston

15. **Which level of government is better able to administer key welfare programs such as Medicaid?**
    a) Federal
    b) State

16. **Should voter ballots and driver's license tests be available only in English?**
    a) Yes
    b) No

17. **Should you be allowed to carry a concealed handgun to protect yourself?**
    a) Yes
    b) No

18. Which of the following "welfare reform" provisions would you support? (Circle all that apply.)
    a) A two-year cutoff for welfare recipients who do not find jobs
    b) Job training and placement for welfare recipients
    c) No additional benefits for welfare recipients with more than two children
    d) Child care to enable welfare recipients with young children to take jobs

19. Which of the following would you support in an effort to cut the U.S. deficit? (Circle all that apply.)
    a) Cut growth of Medicare and Medicaid
    b) Cut loans to college students
    c) Eliminate subsidies to the arts
    d) Cut defense spending

20. Should illegal immigrants be eligible for welfare benefits for their children?
    a) Yes
    b) No

21. Do you approve of the "three strikes and you're out" policy whereby anyone convicted of three felonies would be sent to prison for life without parole?
    a) Yes
    b) No

22. Which statement more closely matches your opinion?
    a) I support the Endangered Species Act because it protects habitat systems.
    b) I oppose the Endangered Species Act because it threatens timber jobs and impinges on private property rights.

23. Should the minimum wage be raised?
    a) Yes
    b) No

24. **Should high schools distribute condoms to students?**
    a) Yes
    b) No

25. **Should sports teams with mascots that offend minority populations change the mascots to more innocuous figures?**
    a) Yes
    b) No

26. **Do you support the death penalty?**
    a) Yes
    b) No

27. **Should the age at which juveniles are judged as adults in criminal cases be lowered to 13 years?**
    a) Yes
    b) No

28. **Should employers be allowed to permanently replace striking workers?**
    a) Yes
    b) No

29. **Should there be a cap on the amount juries can award injured parties?**
    a) Yes
    b) No

30. **How should abortions be restricted? (Circle all that apply.)**
    a) Notify parents before a girl younger than age 18 years has an abortion
    b) No government funding for abortions
    c) Allow abortions only in cases of rape, incest, or danger to the life of the mother
    d) All abortions should be illegal
    e) Abortions should not be restricted

SCORING

Points are added for the liberal answer to each question. The conservative option scores a zero. Tally your score for each question, then add up your total to see where you fall on the political spectrum.

1. a=2 b=0

   Liberals tend to favor an activist government (a) based on the philosophy espoused by founding father Alexander Hamilton, whereas conservatives prefer the smaller government (b) embodied in the views of Thomas Jefferson.

2. a=0 b=1 c=0 d=0

   Conservatives tend to support voluntary prayer in school. Liberals generally support more stringent restrictions on guns and oppose bans on flag burning as an infringement on First Amendment rights. Conservatives tend to support term limits as a check on government power. Liberals tend to oppose them as arbitrary.

3. a=0 b=1

   Liberals like lawyers better; Clancy loads his novels with military hardware.

4. a=0 b=1

5. a=0 b=1

6. a=0 b=1

7. a=0 b=1

   Conservatives would tend to favor tax breaks for corporations, whereas liberals would tend to oppose them.

8. a=0 b=1

9. a=2 b=0

   Conservatives tend to believe U.S. foreign policy should promote national interests. Liberals tend to argue for a foreign policy that also promotes democratic governments and enforces human rights.

10. a=2 b=0

Liberals more often adhere to a strict interpretation of the separation of church and state doctrine, whereas conservatives often believe some overlap between church and state is permissible.

11. a=0 b=1

Tough question, but liberals would more likely put their faith in teachers than would conservatives.

12. a=0 b=2

Liberals tend to argue privacy rights in the case of mandatory HIV testing. Conservatives tend to argue for the greater good.

13. a=0 b=2

Conservatives overwhelmingly support a voucher program for public and private schools. Liberals believe such vouchers would severely harm the public schools.

14. a=1 b=0

This is a no-brainer! Liberals would choose Butch Cassidy over Moses.

15. a=2 b=0

Conservatives choose state governments over the federal government.

16. a=0 b=2

Conservatives tend to favor English as the official language, believing a common language holds society together. Liberals tend to emphasize the multicultural approach, in which society is sensitive to the needs of individuals, including those who do not speak English.

17. a=0 b=1

Conservatives favor "conceal carry" laws, whereas liberals tend to oppose them.

18. a=0 b=1 c=0 d=1
19. a=0 b=0 c=0 d=1
20. a=1 b=0
21. a=0 b=2

Conservatives tend to support tougher sentencing, including the "three strikes and you're out" rule for repeat offenders. Liberals tend to emphasize rehabilitation and contend that "three strikes" laws imprison for life non-violent offenders.

22. a=2 b=0

No sweat on this one. If you're a conservative, you probably favor limiting the Endangered Species Act in favor of jobs. If you're a liberal, you're more likely to put the environment first and to believe that the two goals are not incompatible.

23. a=1 b=0
24. a=1 b=0
25. a=1 b=0
26. a=0 b=1
27. a=0 b=1
28. a=0 b=1

Liberals tend to support unions, which means they oppose companies' being able to hire permanent replacement workers for striking employees.

29. a=0 b=1
30. a=0 b=0 c=0 d=0 e=1

Match your score against our estimates of where these prominent political figures would stand (and the actual score of Rush Limbaugh, who matched our estimate exactly):

40—100 percent liberal (Jesse Jackson)
35—Very liberal (Ted Kennedy)
30—Liberal (Hillary Clinton)
25—Moderately liberal (Bill Clinton)
20—Moderate (Colin Powell)
15—Moderately conservative (Bob Dole)
10—Conservative (Newt Gingrich)
 5—Very conservative (Rush Limbaugh)
 0—100 percent conservative (Jesse Helms)

USA WEEKEND asked its readers to share their scores with us, and 13,690 readers responded to this quiz alone: 6,605 people called a 900-phone line to report their scores, 3,340 people sent postcards and 3,745 took the quiz online, where scores were computed automatically.

Among the respondents, the average score overall was 14.5. Men averaged 11. Women averaged 16.

If you would like to take the quiz online, go to America Online Keyword USA WEEKEND or visit on the World Wide Web http://www. proxima.com/usaweekend. Or you can contact O'Leary/Kamber directly at 3050 K Street, NW, Suite 230, Washington, DC 20007 (202) 944-4855.

3 / The First Time Around

How did you do? Were you surprised by the results? Are you more liberal than you expected? Are you more conservative than you thought? Or did you find yourself avoiding the extremes and landing in the moderate middle of the road?

The test you just took is actually our second "Are You a Conservative or a Liberal?" quiz. The first one ran in *USA WEEKEND* on October 28–30, 1994. You can take that original test in the next chapter, but first let's tell you about the response that it received when it appeared.

The *USA WEEKEND* quiz reached some 19 million households. As we discovered from the letters we received, both through the magazine and at our offices, many of those readers enjoyed the test. Families took it. Law firms took it. Faculty and students at Harvard's Kennedy School of Government took it—and passed it on. Rush Limbaugh took it, as if there was ever any doubt about where he stood politically. And CBN News reprinted our quiz and distributed it as a questionnaire.

The results from the 1994 test accurately predicted the November elections of that year, in which Republicans regained control of both houses of Congress for the first time in four decades. Many of the issues that were covered by the Contract with America—such as term limits and a balanced budget—met with positive responses in our test. The new Republican Party, led by Newt Gingrich, showed a more distinct tilt to the right from the party of George Bush, and Bush lost significant support especially among his base because he pushed through a massive tax increase after promising 'read my lips'.

When we asked readers to share their scores from the 1994 quiz and any resulting discussions, we expected some response, but we didn't expect thousands of letters. So *USA WEEKEND* had to enlist student members of the Society of Professional Journalists at Howard University in Washington, DC to tabulate the responses.

Many scores came with long letters explaining the quiz takers' political views—and, in some cases, taking issue with our arrangement of politicians along the spectrum or our choices of questions. Most readers found the quiz an effective means of measuring their political opinions.

Families took the test together, provoking lively debates over the dinner table. Harley and Terry Sacks of Northampton, Massachusetts, took the quiz with their teenagers. He scored 28, she scored 23, daughter Samantha scored 21, and son Justin scored 8. (Please note that the scoring was the opposite of the 1996 test—a 40 meant 100 percent conservative and 0 meant 100 percent liberal.) "The conversation was at times quite heated and emotional," the parents reported. "The 'ideal America' question created the most controversy." (This question, no. 8, asked, "Do you see the ideal America as an ethnic 'melting pot' in which religious, cultural, and ethnic distinctions are blurred, or as a nation in which ethnically diverse groups ought to coexist while retaining their cultural identity?")

Husbands and wives took the test, and sometimes the results surprised them. One couple told us that the husband had not known his wife was so liberal—and she had no idea he was so conservative. As far as we know, the test has not led to their divorce.

Actually, finding a couple that is split at opposite poles of the political spectrum is somewhat rare. According to the Howard University tabulators, husbands and wives tended to score in the same range—especially if they had been married for a while. But that was not enough for some readers. "My wife and I both scored 37," wrote Dale Yancy of Merrimack, New Hampshire. "We were in a state of depression for the rest of the day that we were not 100 percent conservative! Now we are rereading Rush Limbaugh to find out where we went astray."

Rush Limbaugh himself took the test over a two-day period on his radio show. Although he didn't tally his own score, by our calculations he scored a 37 also. Limbaugh read the test to his almost 20 million listeners so they could take it at home. Limbaugh later complained when our 1996 test ranked him as less conservative than he thought. Our political scale showed him scoring a 5, with 0 being most conservative. When he took the second test (the first was administered across the breakfast table by his wife), he scored a 5. And he later said so on his radio show.

The response from schools and universities was amazing. High school teachers all over the country told us that they had given the quiz to their classes. As we said above, even some faculty and students at Harvard's prestigious Kennedy School took the test. At the University of Central Texas in Killeen, political theory professor Jack Fuller (and the university president, as time permits) gave the quiz to his graduate students, who averaged age 24 years. The average score of his students was 20, smack in the middle of the road, with scores ranging from 6 to 31. But 71 percent of his students scored right of center. Government and business majors scored to the right, whereas social work and psychology majors scored to the left.

Students in Jim Swedenburg's class at Roger Bacon High School in Cincinnati, Ohio, "were surprised to find they were more liberal than they had thought. On the political spectrum you provided, we had one 'Jack Kemp' and a few 'George Bushes,' but the vast majority of students were between 'Hillary Clinton' and 'Colin Powell.'" Swedenburg noted that the students "especially loved the fact that they could all pass a quiz they didn't have to study for."

Although there were quite a few surprising results, most readers appeared to land just about where they expected—which they found reassuring in this age of shifting political labels, party jumping, and complicated social issues with no easy answers. "Imagine my surprise when, with 19 points, I was nearest Colin Powell, the person I would most like to be president!" wrote Agnes Crain of El Paso, Texas. "I would like to see more really capable persons be able to compete in what has now become a money circus."

Although the 1994 test was a fairly accurate indicator of the political mood throughout the country, of course it was unscientific and not meant to predict the future. It was meant mostly for entertainment and edification, so that takers could find out where they and their family, friends, and colleagues stood. We also meant for quiz takers to have some fun taking the test and discussing it afterward.

Most of the issues included in the first quiz are still with us today. Some, like whether former Surgeon General Joycelyn Elders or Pat Robertson is more politically extreme, seem to have answered themselves. Elders was nudged out of office, while Robertson's Christian Coalition played a prominent role in the 1994 elections and 1996 Republican presidential primaries.

Even after a couple of turbulent years, the 1994 test still has remarkable resonance. Liberals and conservatives consistently come down on one side or the other regarding these political controversies. Now take the quiz for yourself and see where you stand.

4 / The 1994 Quiz

See how you do on our first political quiz. For scoring to be valid, you must answer all questions.

1. Generally, do you tend to trust or distrust the government's ability to solve problems?
- ☐ Trust
- ☐ Distrust

2. Which do you trust more?
- ☐ The Pentagon or
- ☐ The Post Office

- ☐ The executive branch or
- ☐ The legislative branch

- ☐ The IRS or
- ☐ The FBI

- ☐ The CIA or
- ☐ The Peace Corps

- ☐ The Joint Chiefs or
- ☐ The United Nations

3. What about private institutions and people. Which do you trust more?
- ☐ Trial lawyers or
- ☐ Doctors

- ☐ Union leaders or
- ☐ Business executives

- ☐ Professional athletes or
- ☐ Team owners

4. The federal government should do more to solve the nation's problems, even if it means higher taxes on: (Check as many as you want.)

- ☐ You
- ☐ Big corporations
- ☐ The wealthy
- ☐ The middle class
- ☐ Small business
- ☐ None

5. Where should government be cut? (Check as many as you want.)

- ☐ Eliminate farm subsidies
- ☐ Eliminate subsidies to the arts
- ☐ Abolish public broadcasting
- ☐ Cut entitlement programs (Social Security, Medicare, etc.)
- ☐ Cut defense spending
- ☐ Reduce welfare spending
- ☐ Reduce foreign aid
- ☐ Keep illegal immigrants from receiving public education
- ☐ Reduce environmental regulation
- ☐ Cut taxes
- ☐ Don't cut at all

6. Which would do more to guarantee competitive elections?

- ☐ Term limits
- ☐ Public financing

7. Who was a better president?

- ☐ Ronald Reagan
- ☐ Franklin D. Roosevelt

8. Do you see the ideal America as an ethnic "melting pot" in which religious, cultural, and

ethnic distinctions are blurred, or as a nation in which ethnically diverse groups ought to coexist while retaining their cultural identity?

☐ Melting pot
☐ Multicultural society

9. **Whose political views do you consider more extreme, those of Surgeon General Joycelyn Elders or the Rev. Pat Robertson?**

☐ Elders
☐ Robertson
☐ Neither

10. **Which would curb violent crime most?**

☐ Stricter controls on the sale of guns
☐ Mandatory sentences for those who use guns in the commission of a crime
☐ Both

11. **In the long run, do you think we can reduce crime more by building more prisons or providing more financial assistance to rebuild our inner cities?**

☐ Build prisons
☐ Rebuild inner cities
☐ Both

Please indicate whether you agree or disagree with each of the following statements.

12. **Even if it means cutting programs, spending must be cut to reduce the federal deficit.**

☐ Agree
☐ Disagree

13. **The federal government is too big.**

☐ Agree
☐ Disagree

14. U.S. interests are more seriously at stake in Haiti than they are in Korea.
    ☐ Agree
    ☐ Disagree

15. Gays and lesbians should be able to marry—or at least be treated as married under law if they so desire.
    ☐ Agree
    ☐ Disagree

16. The news media is dominated by liberals.
    ☐ Agree
    ☐ Disagree

17. The religious right is a threat to our political system.
    ☐ Agree
    ☐ Disagree

18. The federal government should include funds to make abortion services part of any standard benefits package in health care reform.
    ☐ Agree
    ☐ Disagree

19. Deceptive political campaign commercials should be banned.
    ☐ Agree
    ☐ Disagree

20. Graphic pornography should be banned.
    ☐ Agree
    ☐ Disagree

21. As a society, we should spend more money trying to find a cure for AIDS than for cancer and heart disease because AIDS threatens younger people.
    ☐ Agree
    ☐ Disagree

22. Talk radio shows should be regulated to ensure both sides of a debate are represented, because talk radio has an unhealthy impact on the political process.
    ☐ Agree
    ☐ Disagree

23. The breakdown of the traditional American family is the most serious domestic crisis facing our society.
    ☐ Agree
    ☐ Disagree

24. Women and racial minorities should be given preferences in hiring until we achieve true gender and racial equality in America.
    ☐ Agree
    ☐ Disagree

25. Certain environmental problems call for government action, even if it means new programs or increased taxes.
    ☐ Agree
    ☐ Disagree

SCORING

How to assign points:

1. "Trust" gets 0 points. "Distrust" gets 2 points. The major difference between liberals and conservatives is that liberals tend to trust government whereas conservatives do not.

2. Any of the following answers get 1 point (for a maximum of 5 points):
   - The Pentagon
   - The executive branch
   - The FBI
   - The CIA
   - The Joint Chiefs

   Any of these get 0 points:
   - The Post Office
   - The legislative branch
   - The IRS
   - The Peace Corps
   - The United Nations

   Liberals would pick the Post Office, the IRS, the Peace Corps, the United Nations, and the legislative branch because they tend to believe in these institutions.

3. Any of the following answers get 1 point (for a maximum of 3 points):
   - Doctors
   - Business executives
   - Team owners

   These answers score 0 points:
   - Trial lawyers
   - Union leaders
   - Professional athletes

Liberals favor trial lawyers over doctors and workers over executives because they tend to distrust businessmen and favor workers and their advocates.

4. Give yourself 1 point on this question ONLY if you answered "None." All other answers score 0.

5. You get 1 point for every answer (for a maximum of 9), EXCEPT "Cut defense spending" and "Don't cut at all," which score 0.

6. Term limits = 1
   Public financing = 0

7. Ronald Reagan = 1
   Franklin D. Roosevelt = 0

8. Melting pot = 1
   Multicultural society = 0

9. Elders = 1
   Robertson = 0
   Neither = 0

10. Stricter controls = 0
    Mandatory sentences = 1
    Both = 0

11. Build prisons = 1
    Rebuild cities = 0
    Both = 0

12. Agree = 1 Disagree = 0
13. Agree = 1 Disagree = 0
14. Agree = 0 Disagree = 1
15. Agree = 0 Disagree = 1
16. Agree = 1 Disagree = 0
17. Agree = 0 Disagree = 1
18. Agree = 0 Disagree = 1

19. Agree = 0 Disagree = 1
20. Agree = 1 Disagree = 0
21. Agree = 0 Disagree = 1
22. Agree = 0 Disagree = 1
23. Agree = 1 Disagree = 0
24. Agree = 0 Disagree = 1
25. Agree = 0 Disagree = 1

ABOUT YOUR SCORE

Respondents with the most points (40) are 100 percent conservative. Those with the least (0) are 100 percent liberal. Take note: A higher number of points is not meant to imply a higher level of political consciousness! The system of accumulating points for conservative answers is simply a practical method for assigning politically left-to-right slots on the spectrum.

See how you measure up against our estimates of where these prominent political figures would stand. Obviously, there are exceptions, and some might say that other individuals better represent the two points of view. Nonetheless, these examples suggest how most Americans perceive today's political spectrum.

0	100 percent liberal (Jesse Jackson)
5	Very liberal (Ted Kennedy)
10	Liberal (Hillary Rodham Clinton)
15	Moderately liberal (Bill Clinton)
20	Moderate (Colin Powell)
25	Moderately conservative (George Bush)
30	Conservative (Jack Kemp)
35	Very conservative (Bob Dole)
40	100 percent conservative (Ronald Reagan)

5 / Who Are Kamber and O'Leary, Anyway?

Victor Kamber and Bradley O'Leary are veteran political and public relations consultants. If you haven't guessed already, Brad's the conservative and Vic is the liberal. You can bet we disagree on just about everything. But that doesn't keep us from being colleagues, even friends.

Democrat Vic Kamber has always been a liberal. But he started out as a Republican. As implausible as it might sound these days—with the GOP marching in lockstep to the far-right agenda—back when Vic first entered politics, the Republican party had a thriving liberal wing. But when the party started taking its long and hard turn to the right, Vic defected to the Democrats.

As president and founder of The Kamber Group, Inc. (TKG), Vic heads one of the nation's largest independently owned communications consulting and public relations firms. It's also the first and biggest such firm that is unionized.

He launched the firm in 1980 with a staff of two professionals. Today, TKG employs over 100 communications experts who provide a full range of public relations, marketing, advertising, media, graphic design, editorial, and political and strategic consulting services. The firm's clients include labor unions, corporations, trade associations, public interest groups, financial and educational institutions, and political candidates and organizations. Under

Kamber's guidance, TKG has earned hundreds of industry awards for excellence in public relations services and print and audiovisual media products made on behalf of clients.

A prolific writer, Vic is the author of *Giving Up On Democracy: Why Term Limits Are Bad for America* (published in October 1995 by Regnery Publishing), the first book to make the case against term limits. He is currently writing a book on negative political advertising, which is expected to be published in early 1997.

Vic's articles and opinion pieces on contemporary American issues have been published in every leading newspaper in the country. His articles have also been published in a variety of magazines, including *Newsweek, U.S.News & World Report, Advertising Age,* and *Public Relations Quarterly.* Vic is also a frequent contributor to *USA WEEKEND Magazine,* writing numerous point-counterpoint opinion pieces with Brad O'Leary as well as the tests in this book.

Prior to founding his firm, Vic served as assistant to the president of the Building and Construction Trades Department (BCTD), AFL-CIO, where he helped create and carry out programs to enhance the lives of the nearly five million members of its fifteen affiliated unions.

During Vic's BCTD tenure, George Meany, then-president of the AFL-CIO, appointed him director of the AFL-CIO Task Force on Labor Law Reform. Vic had previously served as administrative assistant to Rep. Seymour Halpern (R-NY), where he was responsible for major legislative proposals, press operations, and administration of the congressman's office.

Vic holds a law degree from American University and an LL.M., with highest honors, from George Washington University. He received an M.A. with honors in rhetoric and public address from the University of New Mexico, and a B.A. in history and political science from the University of Illinois.

He was a faculty member of the Georgetown University Business School and has taught law, speech, business, public relations, and campaign management at American University and Howard University. He is a member of the American University President's Circle and has served as national convention chair for the Washington, DC International Convention of Phi Gamma Delta.

Vic is a national vice president of Americans for Democratic Action and serves on the Senior Advisory Board of the American League of Lobbyists. He is a member of the board of directors for the following organizations: the International Foundation for Electoral Systems, which promotes free and fair democratic elections around the globe; Franklin National Bank of Washington, DC; Food and Friends, which provides meals for homebound people with AIDS; and Planned Parenthood of Metropolitan Washington.

Vic is also a member of the Industrial Relations Research Association, Coalition of Labor Union Women, American Civil Liberties Union, Washington Project for the Arts, International Association of Political Consultants, Economic Club of Washington, and the National Press Club. He is also a long-time member of the Newspaper Guild.

Vic is a frequent guest on national and local radio and television commentary and panel debate shows. He has appeared on ABC News's *Nightline,* the *CBS Morning News,* CNN's *Larry King Live,* CNN's *Crossfire,* C-Span, CNBC's *Business Insiders,* the *Fox Morning News,* National Public Radio, and many other programs.

Conservative Brad O'Leary started out as a Democrat and became a Republican in college. He began his career in politics conducting "man on the street" polls for the *St. Louis Globe Democrat* during the 1956 Eisenhower campaign. In 1960, he worked as the only Irish Catholic staff member for Richard Nixon. During the 1960s, Brad was president of the St. Louis Young Republicans and served as deputy campaign manager for state Attorney General Jack Danforth's first U.S. Senate bid. In 1972, Brad was finance director for John Tower's (R-TX) successful U.S. Senate campaign, and brought fundraising to new levels with the first $3 million, 100,000-donor federal campaign.

During the Watergate elections of 1973–1974, while Republicans were being defeated nationwide, Brad served as executive director of the Texas Republican Party. During that time, Texas was the only state that actually gained seats for the party. As national cochairman of Americans for Reagan, Brad played a crucial role in Reagan's election to the presidency.

In addition to his political work, Brad is involved in civic and community activities. He has been working with antidrug programs for more than ten years, and is currently serving as treasurer of Chuck Norris's "Kick Drugs Out of America" program.

For more than thirty years Brad has worked with both national and international refugee organizations for a variety of relief and refugee causes. He helped set up a relief network for the Mujahideen during the war in Afghanistan, and he worked with Bob Hope in administering "The Road to Hope" to aid refugees from Southeast Asia. His involvement in such programs began with establishing a refugee network in Berlin during the 1961 Berlin Wall crisis. He has also worked with Catholic refugee services in

Vietnam, coordinated a Cuban refugee program during the Marielitos crisis, and run an orphanage in Macao in the 1970s.

Brad is former chairman of the board of the American Association of Political Consultants—an organization of the top six hundred Democratic and Republican consulting firms in the United States. Now he is president of PM Consulting, which specializes in public relations/public affairs campaigns and political consulting for corporations and associations. The company has worked on the campaigns of Jack Kemp, Howard Baker, John Tower, Jesse Helms, Strom Thurmond, Phil Gramm, John McCain, and more than one hundred other candidates and organizations. PM has also been active in a number of movie productions, including *Dances with Wolves* and *JFK.*

Brad is the author of two books: *Presidential Follies* coauthored with Ralph Hallow and *Top 200 Reasons Not to Vote for Bill Clinton,* both published by Boru Books.

Together Brad and Vic write the *O'Leary/Kamber Report,* a political newsletter with more than 10,000 readers all over the country. It's a lively and provocative forum, where the left meets the right, and sparks are always flying. The newsletter provides conservative-liberal point-counterpoint arguments on many of the important issues of the day.

The *O'Leary/Kamber Radio Report* is heard each weekend on the NBC Radio Network on over 250 stations. Drawing an audience of some 2 million listeners, it's the fifth most-listened-to political radio show in the country. The hour-long show focuses on one political issue, featuring a debate among four hand-picked advocates, and a lively argument between the two hosts. The advocates range from policy experts to members of Congress to celebrity spokespeople. Recent shows have included such luminaries as House Majority Leader Dick Armey (R-TX) talking about the flat tax; former Senator Howard Metzenbaum (D-OH) on handgun control; Phyllis Schlafly discussing sexual harassment; and *M*A*S*H*'s Mike Farrell arguing against the death penalty.

Brad O'Leary and Vic Kamber are also regularly asked by major periodicals to write columns giving their opposing views on hot political topics of the day. These point-counterpoint articles have been published in a number of different periodicals, including *USA WEEKEND,* which is received by over 19 million households. Chapters 9–15 provide examples of their columns on six issues: social issues, the economy, health care, national defense, politics, and personalities. But before you read about these, learn what is a liberal and what is a conservative.

6 / What Is a Liberal?

BY VICTOR KAMBER

What is a liberal?

Ask fifty liberals and you'll get fifty different answers. That's one reason why liberals have been on the losing side so often lately—we spend more time fighting among ourselves than with our adversaries. But more about that later.

Let me start by offering "Liberalism According to Kamber." A liberal is someone who believes that people become liberated when they are strengthened by the bonds of community, and that true freedom is achieved through—not at the expense of—shared responsibility for our well-being as a people and as a society.

Freedom means the ability to "follow your bliss"; to use one of philosopher Joseph Campbell's favorite terms—to fully realize your creative potential as a human being in your personal and professional life, to pursue happiness, and to improve the quality both of your own life and the lives of others.

By this definition, you cannot be free if you are hungry. You cannot be free if you are consumed with anxiety about your economic future. You cannot be free if you have been "downsized," "outsourced," or "automated" out of a job, and have no new prospects for providing for your family. You cannot be free if you lack health insurance and are one illness away from bankruptcy. You cannot be free if your upstream neighbor pollutes the river that supplies your drinking water. You cannot be free if you are paralyzed by fear of violent crime. You cannot be free if you are denied the means to a college education that would sharpen or unleash your talents. You cannot be free if you face retirement in destitution. You cannot be free if you have no voice in your own workplace.

Hubert Humphrey expressed this concept by saying, "Liberalism, above all, means emancipation—emancipation from one's fears, his inadequacies, from prejudice, from discrimination . . . from poverty." That is why liberals proudly believe that an activist government is essential to preserving and enhancing their freedoms.

Conservatives say that the unfettered marketplace is the best guarantor of freedom and that government is freedom's greatest inhibitor. That may sound right in theory, but it's dead wrong in reality. As Franklin Delano Roosevelt noted, "Economic laws are not made by nature. They are made by human beings." In the years before the Great Depression—and again, in the years since Ronald Reagan became president—it has become clear that, although the free market is a powerful engine for generating wealth, it is inept at distributing wealth, it inhibits the freedoms of too many Americans, and it undermines too many of the values that bind America as a society. "The invisible hand" slaps millions of working families down—which is why the visible hand of government, acting as the agent of the people, is necessary to lift them up.

The unfettered market gave AT&T Chairman Robert Allen compensation worth $16 million and enriched the company's wealthy shareholders 25 percent on their investment last year, while throwing 40,000 hard-working, loyal employees out of a job. The unfettered market gave the top 1 percent of Americans more than 60 percent of all newly created wealth and the top 20 percent of Americans a whopping 99 percent of newly created wealth.

The unfettered market increases productivity without concurrently increasing the wages of the men and women who, by working harder, make their employers more profitable. The unfettered market forces most parents to work longer hours at less pay just to make ends meet, leaving them less time to raise their children, play with them, discipline them, and teach them values. The unfettered market—as the hardly liberal Senator Bob Dole has noted—produces entertainment that glorifies violence and brutality, denigrates women, and portrays sexuality in gratuitous, exploitative fashion before the wide eyes and open ears of children. The unfettered market terrorizes workers with threats of lay-offs, unsafe conditions, dehumanizing employment policies, and intimidation against those who seek to assert their voice through unionization.

Conservatives may believe that slavish devotion to the interests of shareholders is appropriate corporate behavior. But liberals believe that businesses should equally serve the interests of all *stakeholders*—the consumers, the employees, and the communities that are just as critical as investors to corporate success. Conservatives want to retain the profit motive as the sole driving force in American society. But "profit *and* morality are a hard combination to beat," to borrow the words of Humphrey once again.

Liberals believe that government—as the only social institution accountable to all Americans—is the vehicle not for trampling on the market but for taming it, to make it work for working families rather than against them, and to add morality to the decisions of corporate chief executive officers, big-time financiers, Wall Street investment bankers, and other powerful figures who have even more influence on people's lives than politicians. Indeed, government—and private, voluntary associations such as neighborhood organizations, congregations, and labor unions—are the institutions that keep America free from the trials and occasional tyranny of the unfettered market.

Activist government doesn't just serve the people—it also serves the interests of the corporations that reflexively oppose it. That's because any economy that lifts a few yachts while swamping all the rowboats—as the unfettered market does—is destined to drown of its own imbalance or create tidal waves of social upheaval. When government intervenes in the economy on behalf of the people to help reinforce the bonds of community, then all boats rise and all Americans win the freedom to sail in whatever direction their heart leads them.

That is why liberals support a livable minimum wage—so that no one who works full-time has to live in poverty.

That is why liberals support health insurance for all Americans—because no one has the right to life, liberty, and the pursuit of happiness without the right to quality medical care.

That is why liberals insist that Medicare be protected and why they demand that Medicaid be available to Americans living below the poverty level and to middle-income families with a relative needing nursing home care.

That is why liberals support a strong Social Security system—because no one should have to work their tail off for forty-five years only to endure destitution and indignity in retirement.

That is why liberals support trade laws designed to help the employment prospects and living standards of working families, rather than line the already bulging pockets of America's economic elites.

That is why liberals support a strong Occupational Safety and Health Administration—because no one should have to die for his or her job—and strong food safety and inspection programs—because no child should have to die from eating a hamburger contaminated with *E. coli* bacteria. Surely government regulation of business is a small price to pay for saving even one human life.

That is why liberals support environmental laws with real teeth—because pollution of the air, water, and land threatens health, and because the destruction of America's natural heritage leaves the country's fleeting sense of community and nationhood all the more hollow.

That is why liberals support strong antitrust laws—because when just one or even a handful of corporations dominates an industry, competition goes out the window, prices rise, services deteriorate, employees get trampled on, and small businesspeople don't even get the opportunity to enter the market. (One of the ironies of the unfettered market is that, left to its own devices, it eventually destroys competition as monopolies and oligopolies form.)

That is why liberals support regulating tobacco—a product as addictive and deadly as cocaine—to protect children from being seduced by Joe Camel and other sleazy industry attempts to replace the more than 400,000 customers who die every year with those most vulnerable to their appeals.

That is why liberals support expanded aid to education as the key that unlocks a limitless future for children to whom the unfettered market has said, "stay out."

That is why liberals support an approach to welfare aimed at helping recipients gain the tools needed for independence—training, day care, health care—

rather than telling people who never received the essential survival tools in the first place, "Sink or swim; we won't throw you a life raft."

That is why liberals support an approach to crime that puts the greatest emphasis on preventing it from ever happening in the first place—through strict gun control and early intervention in the lives of those most at risk of becoming perpetrators—rather than cleaning up the mess after countless lives have been ruined.

That is why liberals believe that family values cannot be separated from economic values—because it is the financial needs of two-working-parent families and two-job parents that have reduced the time parents can spend with their children and increased the corrosive influence of television in children's lives.

That is why liberals support a progressive income tax, so that those who earn the most from society will give the most back, and those who bear the greatest economic burdens will give the least back.

That is why liberals support economic, fiscal, and monetary policies that benefit Main Street—preserving and creating jobs with good pay, benefits, and career opportunities—rather than those that benefit Wall Street by satiating the demands of country club coupon clippers.

That is why liberals are quickly unifying behind a new proposal offered by Senator Edward Kennedy (D-MA) and supported in principle by Labor Secretary Robert Reich to establish tax incentives for corporations that treat their employees well—provide them with job security, ongoing training, health insurance, and a humane working environment—and behave responsibly toward all their stakeholders.

That is why liberals have always been in the forefront of the civil rights, women's rights, and gay rights movements—because every American has the right to dignity, equal opportunity, and freedom from prejudice.

That is why liberals support proposals to democratize our political process through easier voter registration (The "Motor Voter" law has already raised registration to record levels, with 20 million new voters expected on the rolls by the November 1996 election.) and campaign finance reform that implements public financing, thereby limiting the influence of special interest groups.

And that is why liberals support extending democracy into the economy as well, through labor law reforms that give men and women the opportunity to empower themselves in the work-place through collective bargaining, and end once and for all the pernicious practice of firing workers for exercising their right to strike. Real liberals don't run away from unions—they embrace organized labor as the only institution in America that advances the interests of working families and gives voice to their hopes and dreams.

This gets at the crux of one of the problems facing liberalism over the past decade: the emergence of a virulent strain of elitism. Some purported liberals—who give all liberals a bad name—have actually argued that, from a political standpoint, labor is an albatross; from a personal standpoint, union leaders are dinosaurs; and from a social standpoint, associating with labor is akin to slumming. These people aren't liberals—they're plutocrats.

True liberalism is populist. True liberalism is about empowering ordinary Americans to overcome oppressive economic forces so they can pursue their own destiny—unions being workers' best empowerment tool. True liberalism is about making America a family, a community, in which people take responsibility for both their own lives and decisions, and the lives of others.

Unfortunately, these principles have become lost in the public consciousness as liberalism has been given a bad name. The epithet "LIBERAL!" has become a favorite attack of conservative candidates and a source of terror for spineless, rudderless Democrats. But why?

One reason is that liberalism is identified with big government, and conservatives have become very adept at blaming government for all of America's problems; at the same time, few liberals have bothered to offer any defense, much less a reaffirmation of government's proper role. If you don't argue the point, you lose by default. It's long past time liberals started making the case once again.

Second, liberals have not been effective at making clear that our support of activist government does not mean we never met a government program we didn't like. True liberalism means opposing government pork—from massive spending on defense boondoggles to subsidies for wealthy companies to promote their products overseas to gaping loopholes that allow profitable corporations to pay virtually nothing in taxes—designed by and for special interest groups. True liberals also support innovation and reform in how government operates, and they don't hesitate to favor eliminating or changing programs that aren't achieving their goals. Moreover, true liberals understand the essential role of private voluntary organizations in achieving important societal objectives and believe that intervention by those organizations is preferable to government intervention where possible and appropriate. Thus, the extraordinary success of union apprenticeship programs in the construction industry, to give one example, makes this an area where government can and should stay out.

Third, liberalism has become identified more with social than economic issues. Most—though not all—liberals support abortion rights and reproductive choice. Liberals support civil rights for all minorities—including gays and lesbians, targets of the last remaining form of socially acceptable prejudice. Liberals support separation of church and state, and liberals believe the Bill of Rights is sacrosanct. Liberals must do a better job of making clear to Americans that we support these things because we believe that freedom, tolerance, and diversity are three values that make America the greatest land on Earth. But we must also do a better job of assuring voters that we are second to no one in our commitment to strengthening our families and that we believe morality must guide America's social—and, just as important, our economic—policies.

Fourth, liberalism has been mistakenly identified—primarily through its support for affirmative action—as a philosophy more interested in assuring equal outcomes than equal opportunities. In fact, just the opposite is the case. Affirmative action is needed because people of color and women face discrimination from the time they are born and, as a result, often do not receive the education, health care, nurturance, and support necessary to compete on the same footing as others. Affirmative action seeks to put women and members of minority groups on the same starting line as everyone else—not ahead, as conservatives fallaciously charge, and not behind, which is where conservatives would have them.

Fifth, liberalism has been portrayed as a philosophy that encourages dependence on the federal government. But truly liberal policies do not create dependence—they help people help themselves. Hence, liberals support education—from Head Start to school-to-work programs, from student loans to worker retraining; programs that help lower- and middle-income families own a home; the G.I. Bill, which enabled so many of today's baby boomers to be raised in the middle class; the earned income tax credit, which ensures that people who leave welfare for lower-paying jobs really do get ahead as a result of their hard work; and AmeriCorps, which enables young people to give something back to their communities, gain invaluable experience, and receive college tuition help all at the same time.

Sixth, liberalism has sometimes been painted as anticapitalist. In fact, liberalism saved capitalism in the 1930s, when the horrors of the Great Depression caused other economic and political models—from communism to fascism—to look more attractive to people who had no jobs, money, or hope. If the 1990s' disparities between the rich and everyone else continue to grow—if most working families remain locked out of the new global information economy—we'll see the same phenomenon by the turn of the century. Liberalism is the only economic philosophy capable of smoothing out capitalism's rough edges, of giving it a human face. Liberalism is the best friend that a capitalist with a long-term outlook, an open mind, and a sense of responsibility could ever have.

Of course, most businesspeople might not admit it, but they rely on the federal government as much or more than anyone else. The entire defense industry fed at the public trough for decades, and even after the fall of communism, the Republican Congress still tries to feed it more bacon than it knows how to chew. Other industries, from sugar to tobacco, receive massive federal subsidies. Mining companies, timber companies, and ranchers can use public lands for pennies, ripping off taxpayers while they gouge holes in precious ecosystems.

Whereas these programs are boondoggles, corporate America benefits from legitimate government programs too. Businesses would be nowhere without the massive federal superhighway system and all of the other infrastructure projects funded by the federal government—from bridges to air traffic control, from dams to the broadcast spectrum. Pharmaceutical companies benefit from federally funded medical research. Furthermore, without a steady supply of skilled, capable workers emerging from America's public education system, businesses wouldn't have the person power to compete.

Here again is irrefutable evidence that America needs a strong government and that we are ill-served by conservative efforts to emasculate it. So why have liberals been so woefully ineffective of late? Or, as Russian poet Yevgeny Yevtushenko asked, "Why is it that right-wing bastards always stand shoulder to shoulder in solidarity, while liberals fall out among themselves?"

For one thing, we spend too much time talking to other liberals—either bickering with each other or preaching to the choir. Liberalism must reclaim its populist traditions, rejuvenate its ties to organized labor, and reenergize itself. Liberals must listen better to the American people.

Another problem is money. Multinational corporations and megamillionaires give so generously to the institutions that serve their interests that conservatives have more money than they know what to do with. As a result, they have an astonishing confederation of foundations, think tanks, and action groups and an impressive communications chain among the television talking heads and talk radio gasbags who dominate the media. (If the media is so liberal, then why do conservative talk show hosts outnumber liberal talk show hosts four to one and right-wing columnists dominate the op-ed pages?)

Because conservatives represent the interests of the rich and liberals represent the interests of the middle class and poor, the latter will never be able to match the opposition dollar for dollar. But it's time liberals did a better job of raising money and developing comparable institutions to advance our ideas and programs.

A third problem, ironically, is in liberals' grassroots-level organization. Here, we should overwhelm the conservatives, given that we're on the side of every American who doesn't have a seat in the boardroom, a table at the country club, or a BMW in the driveway. But religious political extremists like the Christian Coalition and other right-wing groups— again, greased by the almighty dollar—have taken a page out of our playbook and outorganized us. That must change—and it is changing. The exceptional work of labor, environmental, women's, senior citizens', community, and minority organizations made the difference in liberal Democrat Ron Wyden's U.S. Senate victory in Oregon earlier this year. The same tenacious political action must be replicated throughout the country from now through November. And with the AFL-CIO making an unprecedented political commitment, it will.

So we liberals have got to get our act together. We must do it in the details, but also in the big picture. We must never again let anyone appropriate liberalism's fundamental values: freedom, family, faith, community, responsibility, and love of country. We must never again let intelligent, activist government go undefended. We must never again run away from the "L-word" as if it stood for leprosy.

Here is what we must do from a positive standpoint:

• Define liberalism ourselves, rather than let conservatives do it for us. I offered one possible definition in the start of this chapter, along with one provided by Hubert Humphrey. Here are two others:

> *The key to the American progressive tradition...has been the view that government's highest purpose is to strengthen the capacities of individuals to achieve self-reliance and to nurture the country's rich networks of civic institutions that are independent both of the state and the marketplace.* (Author and columnist E. J. Dionne, Jr.)

> *Liberalism...is the supreme form of generosity; it is the right which the majority concedes to minorities and hence it is the noblest cry that has ever resounded in this planet. It announces the determination to share existence with the enemy; more than that, with an enemy which is weak.* (Spanish essayist and philosopher José Ortega y Gasset)

• Offer a vision of a better future for all Americans—and their children and grandchildren—one achievable only through liberal policies and a continued key role for government.

• Stay focused on economic issues, especially declining wages and benefits for middle-income families.

• Reintroduce the concept of community into our public discourse. No person is an island, to borrow a cliche, and America cannot function as a society if its only driving force is to "get mine." Whether you live in Westchester County or East Saint Louis, or anywhere in between, your fortunes are tied together. Whether you're the chief executive officer of General Electric or the janitor who cleans the CEO's office—your fortunes are tied together. It's time Americans recognized this and started working to bridge their chasms and bring themselves together. True, people are responsible for their own actions—but they are equally responsible for the welfare of their fellow Americans.

America is a nation founded out of human beings' innate desire for freedom. It remains the freest society on Earth. But as George Bernard Shaw said, "Liberty means responsibility. That is why most men dread it." Conservatives want liberty without responsibility, to have their cake and eat it too. But then it ceases to be liberty and becomes chaos.

Liberalism is the only philosophy that can guarantee Americans' freedom in the truest sense of the word. As the millennium approaches, I believe its time will come again.

7 / What Is a Conservative?

BY BRADLEY O'LEARY

It is difficult to describe in just a few words what a conservative is, because conservatism is not an ideology. In fact, conservatism is the absence of ideology. Conservatives don't have a plan to fix the world; in fact, we are suspicious of such grandiose visions. We are realistic enough to know that human nature is imperfect and are willing to work within the limits of our fallen state, rather than attempting to refashion human beings following the model of some newly developed theory.

Conservatism is the accumulated wisdom of human experience. It is respect for tradition. It is love for family, God, and country. It is skepticism of quick fixes and utopian schemes. It is everything we have learned over the years, often at great cost. The success of America as a country and of Americans as individuals depends on how they apply those lessons—in short, how they put conservative ideas into action.

So what do conservatives believe?

We believe that individuals should be left alone to make their own decisions as much as possible.

We believe that the organic institutions of family, church, and community are better than the created institutions of the state.

We believe that freedom is worth fighting for, or it isn't worth anything.

We believe that each individual has both spiritual and material needs. We try to fulfill both of these deeply rooted human desires without bringing them into conflict. Although we recognize material needs, we do not make a god out of mammon.

We believe in protecting and using our natural resources—conservatives were the first conservationists—in ways that are sensible and just.

We believe that the right to bear arms is necessary to preserve a free and independent nation.

We believe in equality of opportunity, not equality of results.

We believe that the Ten Commandments, and not the Code of Federal Regulations, is the greatest law of man.

We believe that the miracle of life begins at conception, and that abortion is murder.

We believe that true compassion is not paternalism, that those who need help do not require a handout, but a hand up.

In seeking to describe what a conservative is, I have asked some of my conservative friends to submit their thoughts on the subject. Because conservatism is more a deeply personal philosophy than an all-encompassing theory, I felt it would help to pick the brains of these prominent conservatives.

• • •

Paul Weyrich of the Free Congress Foundation agrees that conservatism is not an ideology. To him it's simply a way of life. Paul Weyrich argues that ideologies make statements and that their proponents then expect reality to fit those preconceptions. As Paul Weyrich writes, "*When reality does not obey—and it never does—the ideology demands it be ignored.*" He continues, "*If the ideology gets enough power, it ends up sending the people who dare recognize reality to concentration camps.*"

In contrast to ideology, conservatism starts with what Paul Weyrich calls *"the reality of history."* The lessons that we have learned over time show us the best way to live. Again, Paul Weyrich writes,

> For example, we have learned over hundreds of generations that the family is society's most important institution. The family is where young people are civilized—or not. If the family is weak or broken, then children may grow up barbarous—as some of those in our inner cities have.

Another lesson conservatives acknowledge is that rules are needed. *"Without rules, any society falls apart,"* Paul Weyrich argues. The best rules that humans have yet devised are the Ten Commandments. Not only do conservatives respect the old rules, but we *"are wary of new, untested rules for living, because they often sound good at first but produce unfortunate results. People who throw away the old rules usually end up living sad and wasted lives."*

Paul Weyrich calls the rules a people live by *"culture."* Conservatives are brave enough to point out that not all cultures are equal. Some work better than others. As Paul Weyrich expresses it:

> Western culture is the most successful the world has ever seen, in terms of the good life it offers to the people who are a part of it. That is why we see so many people from other cultures trying to immigrate to Western countries.

Unfortunately, many of those who most enjoy the benefits and protection of Western culture are the first to tear it down. In the 1960s there was a wave of permissiveness, a disregard for the rules of the American culture, and devotion to immediate gratification and moral relativism (the belief that every culture is as good as any other). Paul Weyrich laments the result of these changes: "*What was the best, freest, safest country in the world has turned increasingly into a dangerous and depressing place to live.*"

There is hope, however. America can rebuild its society and make its streets safer, its schools better, its economy stronger, and its families more stable. All this is possible by, in Paul Weyrich's words, returning "*to the solid, proven rules of our Western culture.*"

• • •

Gary Bauer, head of the Family Research Council, writes that a conservative believes in the following (he's careful to point out that these opinions are his own):

1. *The value of experience—and the embodiment of experience in "mediating institutions," entities that play an irreplaceable role in governing community but that are not themselves "government"; e.g., family, church, and voluntary organizations.*

2. *The validity of government—but government that is close to the people, respecting the role and the rights of those "mediating" institutions created by the people.*

3. *Enduring values—the attributes of character that turn raw individuals into faithful spouses, honest workers, and patriotic citizens.*

4. *An even deeper creed—that recognizes that human worth is endowed by the Creator and not by government.*

Gary Bauer points out that conservatives have a passion for history and that many are historians. *"They believe that tradition and the past, and the institutions that have survived the crucible of time, have a claim on our conscience and offer the key to our future."* He remarks that rather than Bill Clinton's campaign song, "Don't Stop Thinking About Tomorrow," conservatives might prefer "Don't Stop Thinking About Yesterday."

By understanding history, conservatives know that conservative ideas and leaders have achieved some great things, particularly in times of crisis. Gary Bauer provides a pantheon of conservative heroes:

- For his courage and his insistence that "religion and morality" are "indispensable supports" to "political prosperity"—George Washington.

- For his insistence on a transcendent creed that decrees no man fit to rule another without the other's consent—Abraham Lincoln.

- For his devotion to limited government and the "small platoons" of community life—Edmund Burke.

- For his belief in political reform, the family, conservation, and a sturdy Americanism—Theodore Roosevelt.

- For his fierce defense of freedom and Western ideals—Winston Churchill.

- For aiding the poor with her personal blood, sweat, and tears—Mother Theresa of Calcutta.

- For their devotion to family, faith, and freedom—millions upon millions of my fellow Americans.

Unfortunately, this last group of heroes is not just being ignored but undermined by liberalism. The family is under siege. Assaulted by economic stress, social upheaval, cultural permissiveness, an ever-growing tax burden, and an increasingly tyrannical government, the American family does not get the respect or the support that it deserves.

• • •

One of the major attacks on the family has been feminism. Liberals have assumed that they speak for all women in their arguments for feminism. But has feminism done anything to "liberate" women? Did they need liberation in the first place?

Beverly LaHaye established Concerned Women for America because she realized that Gloria Steinem, Betty Friedan, and other feminists did not speak for her—or for most women in America. As Beverly LaHaye writes:

Liberal women favor an agenda that sets women apart from men for their own self-interest. They have tried to mimic men, but without giving any favor to men....Conservative women have always appreciated our identity as women and have worked to maintain that identity. We see no need for women to imitate men or compete with men. Men and women are uniquely different.

Although the "feminazis" (as Rush Limbaugh calls them) seek to erase any differences between the sexes, conservatives celebrate those differences and understand them to be the very core of life. Just because women fulfill different roles in the family and society doesn't mean they are less equal than men. Anyone who argues that women can only have power in competition with men in the marketplace and professional realms is underestimating the impact that women have in their traditional roles. Barbara Bush wasn't a lawyer—she didn't insist on being called Barbara Pierce Bush. But she was a greater first lady than Hillary Clinton—more respected, more effective, and a much better role model.

Conservative women believe in timeless, traditional values. According to Beverly LaHaye, *"Our families and our children are our highest priorities."* Liberals and feminists attack traditional moral values, saying that they discriminate against women. *"But the truth is, women, as well as all other Americans, find far more freedom and opportunity through conservative policies than the self-serving interests of liberal feminists."*

This last point is crucial. Who benefits from liberal policies? Do liberals really speak for the American people? Do they even know who these people are? Although some liberals like to characterize conservatives as elitists, in fact, conservatism is a deeply populist and egalitarian philosophy. It is the liberals who are elitist, attempting to coerce ordinary Americans into following their half-baked schemes. Syndicated columnist Linda Bowles reminds us that

> no one did a better job of differentiating between liberals and conservatives than did

Thomas Jefferson. In 1824 he wrote the follow-
ing in a letter to a friend, Henry Lee: 'Men by
their constitutions are naturally divided into two
parties: (1) Those who fear and distrust the peo-
ple, and wish to draw all powers from them into
the hands of the higher classes. (2) Those who
identify themselves with the people."

If Jefferson were alive today, he would look at
the elitist liberals who try to micromanage every
American's affairs and see a class that distrusts the
people. He would see conservative populists like
Rush Limbaugh and Newt Gingrich as leaders who
identify with the people.

How do these opposing impulses translate into
power politics? The liberals seek to accumulate all
power in the federal government. As P. J. O'Rourke
said in his review of Hillary Clinton's book, "*It takes*
a village to raise a child. You are the child. And the
village is Washington." Conservatives believe that
whoever is closest to a problem has the most
effective means of solving it. That means power
should be devolved to the lowest possible level—
to the individual, the family, the community. Only
when these entities cannot address a problem
effectively should it be dealt with by the state. The
solution should always be sought at the closest
levels of government: first local government, then
state government, and, only in last resort, the federal government.

Today people are angry and frustrated with the
government precisely because the liberals have
made it take on powers that it is incapable of
administering fairly or effectively. A 1995 Gallup poll
showed that 39 percent of Americans believe that
"the federal government has become so large and

powerful it poses an immediate threat to the rights and freedoms of ordinary citizens." These are not militia members, but ordinary Americans who are responding to a government grown out of control.

We are drowning in our own laws. Regulations in the *Federal Register* now number some 65,000 pages. All these volumes of regulations stacked together would reach the top of the Washington Monument. The *National Review* makes the point that there are 66 words in the Lord's Prayer, 286 in the Gettysburg Address, 1,322 in the Declaration of Independence, but 26,911 words of regulations on the sale of cabbages.

• • •

Liberalism used to fight tyranny. Now it is tyranny. When first developed as a political philosophy, liberalism meant freedom and minimal government. As Keith A. Fournier of the American Center for Law and Justice remarks:

> *Classical liberals fought for free markets, free speech, and limited government. Lord Action —a 19th century liberal of this persuasion—still stands as a giant to all who cherish religious and economic liberty. Ironically, his contemporary admirers are now called "conservatives."*

And what about the people we now call "liberals"? Keith Fournier continues:

> *The "liberalism" of today is in reality nothing more than a disguised statism. Its credo is more akin to the French Revolution than to the philosophy of those who founded America....We must never forget that a centralized bureaucratic government is part of what our ancestors fled....*

Jean-Jacques Rousseau is purported to have said that "the first face a newborn child should see is the state." Today's "liberal" regime is a fulfillment of Rousseau's vision. The state has become the new "family" and every citizen is now dependent on it.

Where once it used to be the banner of freedom, liberalism now means servitude to the state. As Linda Bowles writes:

Clearly, new-age liberals are not liberal at all in the classic sense, but control freaks. While passionately rejecting the idea that anyone has the right to impose values upon anyone else, they rush to impose their own ideological folly and cultural prejudices upon others.

The tyranny of liberalism has been one long record of failure, throwing money and resources at problems that, paradoxically, only get worse. But beyond liberalism's noted failure is the question of whether its assumption of power was even legal. *"It would be difficult, probably impossible, to find constitutional roots for most of what our government is doing these days,"* Linda Bowles writes. *"The government has declared itself, rather than the people, the centerpiece of a 'reinvented' America —by preempting private business, the individual, the family, parents, the church, even God himself."*

The Founding Fathers saw the government as a way to protect life, liberty, and the pursuit of happiness. Note that they did not promise that government would guarantee happiness. The liberal state seeks to enforce happiness by edict. No wonder so many people are unhappy.

Linda Bowles argues, "*We have strayed far from the two basic principles which guided the Founders: the principle of limited government which empowers the people, and the principle of moral responsibility which makes that empowerment possible.*"

The liberal state has not only tyrannized the people, but crippled their moral sense. When people are no longer in charge, they are no longer responsible for themselves and for others. No wonder the rise of the liberal state and liberal ideology has corresponded with a rise in irresponsibility and the breakdown of family and community. When the federal government is making all your decisions for you, it's difficult to develop any sense of moral agency. In a world where almost everything is regulated, all that is not regulated is permitted.

This century's lessons should have taught that moral responsibility is undermined by the powerful central state. The totalitarian dictatorships of Hitler and Stalin were filled with murderers who were just following orders. Although not every liberal is a Hitler or a Stalin, it must be remembered that those dictators believed that what they were doing was in the best interest of their people and their nation.

The twentieth century has been a time of dizzying change and catastrophe. Conservatives, in the words of William F. Buckley, "*Stand athwart history yelling 'Stop!'*" Although we realize that we cannot turn back the clock and return to less troubled, less complicated times, we seek to preserve what is good about the past and try to restore what has been lost in this century's tragic enthusiasm for progress.

What has gone wrong? People haven't changed. But the state has. Syndicated columnist and talk show host Armstrong Williams points out this difference between people and the state:

People balance their checkbooks and they wonder why the government does not. People prioritize their resources and make hard decisions and they wonder why government does not. People wonder why partisan sides cannot put aside their differences, find a compromise and agree to act together.

Again, conservatives are on the side of people, whereas liberals take the side of the state. Armstrong Williams continues,

Unlike liberals, who believe government to be the panacea for all societal problems, conservatives still have faith in the power of the individual. Conservatives have watched as liberals have wasted billions of dollars on government programs that have done nothing more than exacerbate the problems they were initiated to confront.

This is the law of unintended consequences—when an attempt by government to fix a problem beyond its grasp not only fails to solve the problem, but creates new and unexpected ones. This can be seen in the war on poverty, where the $5 trillion spent on welfare has only created more poverty. It has broken up poor families, created an almost exponential growth in illegitimacy, and established a seemingly permanent underclass.

This is how Edwin Feulner of the Heritage Foundation characterizes the law of unintended consequences, and conservatives' suspicion of easy schemes:

We recognize that the world will always be a troublesome place. We can make it better—

but if we try to make it perfect, we'll almost always make it worse.

But that doesn't mean conservatives are unwilling to attempt reasonable solutions. "*Just because conservatives don't go along with such schemes doesn't mean we don't care about solving problems,*" Ed Feulner writes. He continues:

It doesn't mean we're happy with injustice or unwilling to help eradicate it wherever possible. Rather it means we believe the best way to attack problems is to recognize human failure and frailty for what it is, take slow, measured, prudent steps toward solving problems that can be solved, and watch the results closely so we learn what works and what doesn't—and adjust our actions accordingly.

Whereas conservatives take this judicious approach to problems and attempt to enhance what is good in society, "*the liberal crusader is focused on the negative. He is trying to stamp out all evil with the coercive hand of big government, and winds up destroying much of what is good in the process.*"

The conservative goal is not some utopia (Greek, meaning no place), but what Russell Kirk called "*a tolerable, civil social order.*" To achieve that order, conservatives offer a reasonable and responsible political program, keeping in mind the limits of politics. Armstrong Williams describes the conservative alternative thus:

Conservatives maintain that the problems facing our families, the problems facing our

*schools and the problems facing our neighbor-
hoods can and should be solved by our families, schools and neighborhoods—not faceless
bureaucrats in government agencies.*

According to Armstrong Williams, it comes down to
trust.

*Conservatives trust people and their neighbors
to solve most of their problems, while liberals
believe most people are unable to act responsibly without government direction.*

But conservatism is about more than just the
government and politics. Bill Murchison, a syndicated columnist based with the *Dallas Morning
News*, writes, "*Over the past sixty years we have
grown used to defining ourselves by our political
commitments, as if politics were the most important occupation on earth.*" Conservatives understand that politics is just one aspect of life—
necessary and perhaps crucial, but still only part
of the picture. As Bill Murchison notes:

*Government isn't spirit, it's flesh and metal and
paper. Hearts, souls, minds, the things that
inform behavior and ultimately shape what we
call the quality of life—such things are beyond
the government.*

Conservatives are skeptical of government not
just for the practical reason that much of what
government does is ineffective or actually harm-
ful, but also because we understand the limits of
government and politics. To a great extent this
larger understanding comes from our religious
convictions. Conservatives believe that the role
of religion—not just in our private lives, but in the

public sphere—is essential. Again, turning to Armstrong Williams:

> *Unlike liberals who believe that religion has little place outside a church, a synagogue or home, conservatives believe that religion has a fundamental place at the center of the public square.*

Conservatives believe in freedom of religion. No one respects the rights of other religions to worship freely more than American conservatives. We know that this country was founded on religious tolerance and built by people of many different faiths. By insisting with specious legalistic reasoning that public life be entirely bereft of religious words and symbols, liberals have done more than simply separate church and state. They have evacuated from public life any deeper meaning. Now Americans no longer have a common faith in God. They are supposed to replace that with faith in the government. Liberals insist on a separation of church and state because they are afraid that religious belief threatens the one power they do believe in—the state. Conservatives understand that religion is the cornerstone of a moral order and an essential aspect of an orderly and humane public life.

That does not mean conservatives want everybody to believe as we do, or that we insist on their believing at all. We only ask that the spiritual life not be treated as if it were something shameful or outdated. Freedom of religion can exist only where there is respect for religion. The federal government subsidizes blasphemous art while insisting that Christmas Nativity scenes are unconstitutional. Liberals have embarked on a secular jihad that is as intolerant and uncompromising as any holy war. As Armstrong Williams writes,

> *For conservatives there is no limiting God. We are all sons and daughters of the Almighty. Our ability to do good, act compassionately, demonstrate understanding, practice charity, place the needs of others before ourselves— comes from God. The very best that we can be and the very best that we can do cannot be separated from our religious faith....*
>
> *Conservatives want to see this nation and our public life reflect the virtues and values that germinate from a life of faith. Conservatives do not want to see religious prejudice. Conservatives do not want to see anyone forced to believe or act in a manner that threatens their heritage or conscience.*
>
> *However, conservatives do want to see a nation that respects the difference between right and wrong. Conservatives do want to see a nation where decency has meaning and moral corruption is not rampant.*

• • •

Conservatives recognize that liberty is not license, but responsibility. Pope John Paul II has reminded us that "*freedom does not consist in doing what we want, but choosing to do what we ought.*" Phyllis Schlafly, president of Eagle Forum and syndicated columnist, puts it in more pungent, partisan terms: "*A liberal is someone who is liberal with other people's money and other men's wives.*" The two are not unrelated. A breakdown in moral responsibility has corresponded with a rise in government power. Total government spending now takes up some 36 percent of gross domestic product (GDP). Around the turn of the century, government accounted for only about 10 percent of GDP.

Who's paid for all that government growth? American families. According to the Institute for Policy Innovation, the average American household had a tax burden of $1,370 in 1900. By 1995 that burden had increased to almost $20,000! The average family works until May 5 of every year just to pay its tax bill. Taxes are now overwhelmingly the largest portion of household expenditures. The average family spends as much in taxes as it does on housing, food, medical care, and clothing combined. And what has the average American family enjoyed in return for that enormous increase in taxation? Very little.

So who has benefited from all these government programs? Not the poor. Poverty began declining during the 1950s and early 1960s. Then along came the Great Society, and the poverty rate leveled off, even increased somewhat, despite the government's throwing trillions of dollars at the problem. And as welfare spending continues to increase, the ranks of the underclass continue to grow.

Welfare has broken up families, creating both social chaos and economic need. Before the Great Society programs, 7.7 percent of babies were born out of wedlock. Today illegitimacy has climbed to 28 percent of all births. The poverty rate for traditional families is five per one thousand, while the poverty rate for single-parent families is eight times higher. Since 1970, the number of children living in poverty has increased 40 percent.

The liberal state rewards bad behavior and punishes good behavior. Work hard, pay your bills, pay your taxes, and try to raise a family, and you will get very little from the liberal state. But if you're a criminal, if you refuse to work, or if you find some way to prove that you are a victim of society, you will be rewarded. Meanwhile, the people who built this country, whose hard work and honest living have made America the envy of all other nations, get nothing but higher taxes and a more intrusive government. No wonder people are angry and want change.

Still, that change has to be wrought out of thoughtful and selfless devotion to the greater common good. There is no room in the conservative movement for haters or extremists. People who pursue violent and illegal methods are not true conservatives—they do not want to conserve anything, they only seek to destroy. The conservative vision is not a negative agenda. We offer not only a critique of the failed policies and destitute ideas of liberalism, but a positive alternative. As Keith Fournier writes, *"We stand in a millennial moment."* He continues:

> It is time for a new generation of leaders to lay a foundation of freedom for the future, a dynamic conservatism that points the way toward a new safety net consisting of private sector solutions which promote capitalism with a conscience and demonstrate that there is no conflict between compassion and competition.

Conservatives believe that the marketplace is economic democracy—free people making their own decisions unencumbered by political power or the crude interference of the state. But we realize that the market is not all. Although conservatives believe that material prosperity is important for a democratic republic, we also understand that money is not the measure of man. Instead we have other needs and other values. A just society is a prosperous society. But not every prosperous society is just.

By making a God out of material things, people neglect the God that lives within them, and their lives become tawdry enterprises. The vacuity of consumer culture is to a large extent the result of a spiritual impoverishment. By relegating God to the margins, people have lost His redeeming grace. They have become bodies without spirit, adrift in the material world. This is but one price of liberal progress.

Conservatives are not opposed to progress. We're not against change. In fact, we think that our country needs change. But instead of leading the nation toward the uncharted waters of fashionable ideas, we would like to guide it back toward the safe harbor of proven wisdom. Family, God, and country are what made America great. And a return to these values can make America great again.

8 / Point-Counterpoint

Political issues usually offer two stark choices, roughly corresponding to liberal and conservative alternatives. Sometimes liberals and conservatives agree about a particular problem, but have profound disagreements about proposed solutions. For example, everyone wants a strong economy—but liberals and conservatives often differ on how best to achieve it. Other times they disagree even on the conception of the problem itself. For example, in the health care debate, liberals pointed to the health care crisis as reason for adopting the Clinton plan, whereas conservatives maintained the position there was no health care crisis to begin with.

The currency of a democracy is words. Proponents make arguments and hope to convince their opponents. The way an issue is framed is extremely important to political debaters. Sometimes even the terminology used in the course of an argument can cast that argument in a particular light. Were the Contras "freedom fighters" or "terrorists"? Was Reagan's strategic defense initiative "Star Wars" or a "Space Shield"? These are not mere semantic distinctions; they reveal a fundamentally different conception of the issues.

Liberals see things one way, and conservatives see them another. Show them both the same economic data and they may draw different conclusions. Liberals are more concerned with unemployment and wage disparity. Conservatives care more about economic expansion. Looking at the glass of America's political state, liberals may see it half empty, whereas conservatives may call it half full—or the other way around, depending on the issue.

This opposition is essential to a vibrant democracy. Liberals and conservatives may agree on very little; some of them might not even like each other (though we believe that you can be very serious about politics without taking it personally; in fact, political adversaries can often become great friends). But liberals and conservatives need each other to ensure a spirited debate and provide meaningful choices to the voters. This is the dynamic of democracy, the constant peaceful conflict between two opposing forces that are committed to a common good and are willing, eventually, to compromise. That's how Americans make laws and govern their country.

Democracy is about argument. And we have made something of a career out of arguing with each other. We regularly publish opposing point-counterpoint columns in *USA WEEKEND, Paradigm 2000,* and *The O'Leary-Kamber Report.* These columns cover some of the most important issues debated over the past several years. Many of the same issues are still being debated today. Chapters 9–15 contain a selection of the arguments that we have had over the years. Next to the subject we have provided the year the columns were published.

9 / Social Issues

Nowhere is the liberal/conservative split more evident than in social issues. Social issues are that broad and controversial strata of concerns about our private lives. In general, liberals prefer a more free and open approach to personal issues, while conservative seek to enforce a stricter moral code governing our behavior.

One of the hottest social issues is abortion. Most conservatives believe that abortion is murder. Most liberals think otherwise and that a woman should have the right to control her own body.

We have our own strong opinions on the issue. Here's how we weighed in after the Supreme Court's *Webster* decision, which gave the states greater authority to restrict abortions.

ABORTION (OCTOBER 1989)

ABORTION IS MURDER
BY BRADLEY O'LEARY

I, and 91 million other Americans, firmly believe that the 1.5 million abortions committed last year due to economic factors—and worse, simple inconvenience—were murders.

While the 91 million who find abortions morally unacceptable recognize that there are justifications in the abortion of a fetus—rape, incest, life-endangering medical crises—we also recognize that these justifications account for less than 5 percent of the abortions in the country.

We are willing to vote for our convictions and at the ballot box are often joined by an additional 14 million Americans who believe that even though many economic conditions may justify abortion, factors such as social inconvenience do not.

Americans, by overwhelmingly insisting abortion is a euphemism for murder, have shifted the arguments away from the calculating technocracy of Supreme Court Justice Blackmun's arbitrary chronology to arguments supporting the value of life versus rationalizations for the termination of that life.

We are opposed by almost 45 million Americans united with groups such as the National Organization for Women (NOW) and the National Abortion Rights Action League (NARAL), who believe abortions are morally right under any circumstances.

Polls indicate the strength of commitment tends to vary between individuals making up both pro-life and pro-choice groups, and because of this variance, Democratic candidates are paying a price at the polls. There are about 10 million Democratic pro-lifers likely to cross party lines in an election because of this single issue, while there are 4 million pro-choice Republicans who would switch parties.

The Democratic Party, because it has made this issue an integral part of its national platform, has more at stake than the GOP, whose candidates are free to make their own choice without being hung with the albatross of the national party's special interest commitments.

The Webster decision energized NOW and other pro-choice forces into mobilization. Despite this mobilization, there have been three congressional elections and three pro-choice losses.

Pro-life victories in Florida, Texas, and California suggest the problems faced by the pro-choice movement. These elections were clear indications of how the rallies and marches favored by NOW and NARAL are difficult to translate into victories at the ballot box.

As more short-term losses cement the long-term situation, the pro-choice movement will find itself relying more and more on NOW, pushing itself even further out of mainstream American politics, and eventually moving outside even the mainstream of the Democratic Party.

KEEP ABORTION SAFE AND LEGAL
BY VICTOR KAMBER

It's a sad fact of political life that there are always those who would turn back the clock on some of the great social advances of our times.

One of those advances was the Supreme Court's ruling in *Roe v. Wade* that government should stay out of the most profoundly personal choice a woman can make—whether to carry a pregnancy to term.

How ironic that the ultimate legacy of Ronald Reagan, the man who promised to get government off our backs, is a Supreme Court that sticks government's large and unsightly nose into the personal lives of millions of women.

Isn't the "laissez faire" philosophy of Reagan and Bush more applicable than ever on the issue of abortion? There is no religious or moral consensus on the question of abortion. In the absence of such a consensus, the only appropriate government response is to allow choice. And on a practical basis, government policy that would make millions of decent women criminals or force them to get life-threatening, back alley abortions is morally repugnant.

Most Americans share this view. Poll after poll demonstrates that two of every three Americans support keeping abortion legal.

In the past, most pro-choice voters were complacent and did not cast their ballots according to the candidates' positions on abortion, while anti-abortionists were much more likely to be single-issue voters.

But the Supreme Court's *Webster* decision, which allowed states to restrict abortion, turned this situation on its head. Members of the pro-choice majority, recognizing that this fundamental right is endangered, are going to be much more likely to vote for the pro-choice candidate, regardless of party. The opportunity for gain by the anti-choice minority is smaller, since more already vote on a single-issue basis.

We've already seen this phenomenon in heavily ethnic, Catholic New Jersey, where pro-choice Democratic gubernatorial candidate Jim Florio has built a double-digit lead over Republican Jim Courter. Courter had a 100 percent anti-abortion voting record in the House, but faced with the furor of public opposition to the *Webster* decision, he said as Governor, he wouldn't recommend legislation to outlaw abortion.

Pro-choice candidates have been trumpeting their position on abortion. Anti-choice candidates have either been backpedaling or uncharacteristically silent.

We can expect to see many middle-income, suburban, independent swing voters leaving the Reagan/Bush coalition, and joining a newly dominant, largely Democratic, pro-choice coalition electing like-minded candidates at all levels of government.

• • •

Liberals and conservatives are bitterly divided over the role of religion in our public life. Liberals generally support a separation of church and state as the best guarantor of religious freedom. Conservatives argue that rigid separation too often keeps deeply-held religious beliefs—and hence morality—too far removed from political life and policy decisions.

Conservative religious organizations emerged in the late 1970s to become a potent force in electoral politics. Liberals think these groups are intolerant hate-mongers. Conservatives think they are providing necessary moral ballast to our ship of state. Here's what Kamber and O'Leary have to say about the Religious Right.

THE RELIGIOUS RIGHT (OCTOBER 1994)

GIVING CHRISTIANITY A BAD NAME
BY VICTOR KAMBER

Whenever I hear Jerry Falwell, Pat Robertson and their apologists in the Republican Party accuse Democrats of "religious bigotry" for criticizing the so-called "religious right," my stomach turns.

You see, my father was a Pentecostal Minister who, along with my devout mother, gave me a strict, fundamentalist Christian upbringing. I was taught from day one to love thy brother. I was taught to treat all human beings with respect and dignity—that we are all creations of God. I was taught to forgive others' errors because we are all imperfect. I was taught the virtue of humility. And I was taught that hard work and living the right way would bring the ultimate reward—going to heaven—with secular concerns and materialism taking a back seat.

I look at Falwell, Robertson, and their ilk and see nothing in common with my father. Rather than love, they preach hate. Rather than treat all people as God's creation, they equate their political opponents with the devil. Rather than forgiveness, they practice vindictiveness. Rather than show humility, they indulge in brazen ego gratification. And rather than eschew materialism, they have made themselves shamelessly wealthy.

They're giving evangelical Christianity, the religion my father preached, a bad name. Shame on them.

They are disingenuous in charging that Democrats who attack their politics are attacking their religion. For Robertson, Falwell, et al., are not using politics to advance an agenda based on religious values, something done honorably by people of many faiths in this country's history—they are using the cloak of religion to advance an extremist political agenda and raise millions of dollars. This is the work of charlatans and swindlers.

Where in the Bible does it even remotely imply that a government should not provide health care coverage for all of its citizens? Yet Robertson's Christian Coalition claims that President Clinton's health care reform plan was somehow morally wrong. My interpretation of the Bible, gained from my evangelical father, suggests that Jesus would look kindly on the notion of a people acting to protect the health and well-being of their brothers and sisters. But I'm not arguing I'm a better judge of the Bible—just that health care reform is a political battle. To mask it in the language and symbols of religion is a sleazy, malevolent ruse.

And how is it consistent with the values of evangelical Christianity for Falwell to peddle a videotape that makes vulgar, slanderous and false charges that

President Clinton is guilty of murdering people? Did Falwell gain a divine exemption from the Ninth Commandment, "Thou shalt not bear false witness against thy neighbor"? For this man to claim that he speaks for God or Jesus Christ is an obscenity.

Falwell and Robertson also use the old ploy that their critics "are really attacking our followers." Having grown up not just among my family but my father's congregation, I have the greatest respect for the decency and integrity of evangelical Christians, and the greatest empathy for their longing for a return to traditional values in these times of precipitous change and apparent moral decline. But their fears and yearnings are being cynically manipulated by the religious right's leaders to advance partisan political ends of which they may not be fully aware—and may not fully support.

I would be shocked if many Christian Coalition members endorsed Pat Robertson's statement characterizing feminism as "a socialist, anti-family political movement that encourages women to leave their husbands, kill their children, practice witchcraft, destroy capitalism, and become lesbians."

I don't believe many evangelicals equate the Episcopal, Methodist, and Presbyterian churches with "the spirit of the anti-Christ" as Robertson did on his show, *The 700 Club.*

And I cannot accept that many conservative Christians are so intolerant as to believe, as Robertson has said, that their political opponents are "satanic forces"—not just "human beings to beat in elections."

Just as appalling as the extremism and intolerance of Falwell and Robertson is the Republican Party's attempt to have its cake and eat it too. Behind the scenes, the GOP works closely with the religious right, hoping to gain from the "stealth" and "guerilla war-fare" strategies advanced by Christian Coalition exec-utive director Ralph Reed. The National Republican Senatorial Committee even provided the Christian Coalition's first seed money. The GOP helps the religious right to turn their voters out to the polls to vote a party-line ticket. But they are trying to keep their efforts under wraps—because they know that the moderate subur-banites and Reagan Democrats that are the key to Republican Party success are repulsed by the extrem-ism and intolerance of Falwell and Robertson.

However, the camel's nose is now firmly ensconced under the tent. An estimated eighteen state Republican Parties are now controlled or largely influenced by the radical right. So the next sound you hear may be the stampede of moderate swing voters leaving the GOP in droves. The takeover is so complete that Senator Arlen Specter (R-PA) was roundly booed at the Iowa Republi-can presidential cattle show for making the blasphe-mous statement that he supported the separation of church and state.

This should give any Catholic, Episcopalian, Methodist, Presbyterian, Jew, Muslim or member of any faith other than that practiced by Falwell, Robertson and their clones reason for pause. If the religious right ever got its way, the right to practice the religion of one's choice free of government inter-ference might be the first thing to go.

It's time for Americans of all faiths and all political persuasions to condemn and discredit our modern-day Elmer Gantrys, Jerry Falwell, and Pat Robertson.

A MAINSTREAM FORCE
BY BRADLEY S. O'LEARY

President Clinton and his liberal spokespeople California Congressman Vic Fazio, Surgeon General Joycelyn Elders, consultant Frank Greer, and Democratic National Committee Chairman David Wilhelm—who speak for the religious left—have begun the battle against American mainstream values. "Intolerant!," "Extremist!," "Bigoted!" are but a few of the political salvos fired by Clinton and the religious left, who seek to weigh America's moral anchors.

Groups like the Christian Coalition have been vilified for straying far outside the religious arena by tackling such issues as taxes, education, health care, abortion, and homosexuality. What the "left" fails to recognize is that these are family values, and it's no surprise that President Clinton fails to grasp the meaning of "family values" because those two words are but a political catch-phrase to him. The concerted effort by Bill Clinton and the religious left to portray the religious right as an evil cabal set on converting the nation to extreme conservatism does nothing but speak to their ignorance, elitism, and intolerance!

Far from some radical sect of wild-eyed, Bible-thumping conservatives, the religious right consists of average Americans who are fed up with the Clinton administration's vision for our country and the continual assault by government institutions on their faith. They represent a broad mix of Americans who resent the Clinton administration's efforts to foist upon them the homosexual lifestyle, unconditional abortions paid for by the federal government, condom distribution in schools, the empty promise of tax relief, and the continual assault on religion by the U.S. Supreme Court.

Clintonites have this argument backwards. The religious right is a majority of Americans defending their traditional beliefs against continual assaults from a minority that seeks to substitute their immoral and amoral values for those that made our country great. The religious left, for their part, are a rich, mobile, and highly vocal minority group in American politics. Recent polling data seems to make this case:

- A Times Mirror poll conducted in July showed that 53 percent of all Americans think moral problems are more important than economic problems. Only 31 percent felt that American families are threatened more by economic strains. The religious right is leading the charge to restore America's moral fiber while the religious left seeks to accommodate homosexuality, abortion and pornography.

- According to a *Los Angeles Times* news story on the poll, Americans display a greater concern about the political influence of culturally divisive groups associated with the Democrats. Nearly 40 percent of Americans felt that liberal groups like feminists and gay activists were a greater threat to society, while only 12 percent of Americans named conservative religious groups.

- The July Times Mirror poll also showed that 71 percent of Americans think the traditional family structure is always best, while only 28 percent of Americans disagreed. The religious right favors a traditional family structure while the religious left condones same-sex marriages.

- Nearly 70 percent of Americans in the *Los Angeles Times* poll oppose the inclusion of insurance coverage for abortions in any basic health care legislative proposal. Only 45 percent of Americans favor legalized abortion in the poll, yet the Clinton administration sought to have this included in health care reform.

- More than two-thirds of Americans, especially those who make up the religious right, think that homosexual relations are always wrong—yet only 18 percent of Americans, including the religious left, felt that homosexual relations were not wrong. Despite the minority of Americans who feel that homosexual relations are okay, there were no charges of undue influence from the media about the 100-plus openly gay delegates to the Democratic National Convention nor the $13 million raised by the gay community for Bill Clinton's presidential campaign.

- The religious right opposes the legalization of marriages between homosexuals—a view that is shared by 64 percent of Americans according to a *Time*/CNN poll conducted last June. Only 3 in 10 Americans support legalized marriages between homosexuals. The Clinton administration, beholden to the gay lobby, has voiced no opposition to such marriages.

- More than half of Americans favor condom distribution in public schools in a recent NBC News/*Wall Street Journal* poll. A nearly equal number of Americans, 46 percent, and most members of the religious right oppose condom distribution in schools, yet religious left spokesperson Surgeon General Joycelyn Elders advocates and promotes condom distribution in public schools.

- The religious right has fought lock and step with most Americans to stamp out illegal drugs. Thirty-seven percent of Americans favor locking up sellers and users. Another 30 percent favor at least jailing the seller. However, only 13 percent of Americans favored legalizing drugs, yet religious left spokesperson Elders thinks that this, too, is a great idea.

- Prayer in public schools is not only championed by the religious right but by 76 percent of Americans in a recent *Los Angeles Times* poll. Opposition to school prayer from the religious left and other Americans accounted for only 20 percent of the responses. President Clinton favors prayer only at sporting events and graduation ceremonies in large places.

- A 1990 NBC News poll showed that 54 percent of Americans felt there should be restrictions on National Endowment for the Arts grants to artists who produce art some people consider obscene. The religious right has long sought to restrict taxpayer-funded obscenity such as the Mapplethorpe exhibit. The religious left opposes any restrictions—a view shared by only 38 percent of the public.

- The religious right has sought tax relief for the average American family. Despite claims by President Clinton to have eased the tax burden on families, a *Time*/CNN poll shows that 65 percent of Americans still feel they pay too much in taxes. Members of the religious left continue to look to new taxes as a means of feeding the government spending machine. Incidentally, only 32 percent of Americans feel that the amount of taxes they pay is appropriate.

- A March CNN poll showed that only 25 percent of Americans think that conservative Christian groups have too much influence in the Republican Party. An October 1990 CNN poll showed that 48 percent of Americans felt unions had too much influence in government. In 1992, one-third of delegates to the Democratic National Convention were union members, and yet organized labor is not attacked by the media for their "evil" influence.

It's clear from these poll results that the "religious right" shares its values with mainstream America, while Bill Clinton and the religious left are still peddling values that just don't wash with the average American.

There is only one reason why President Clinton, Wilhelm, and Fazio are demonizing the religious right. They are scared stiff by the prospect of America's 137 million Christians uniting behind a party and a candidate that still share their values. The only way the religious left can hope to shut down this growing force is to portray them as an extremist, intolerant and bigoted group.

Christian conservatives have become politically active with the help of groups like the Christian Coalition because they are fed up with Clinton's twisted vision for America. They're fed up with educrats trying to dumb-down their public schools, courts that must decide if wearing a cross in the workplace constitutes harassment, the legitimization of homosexuality and abortion, taxpayer-funded obscene art, big government intrusion into our daily lives, taxes that penalize marriage, phantom middle-class taxcuts, administration figures who advocate the legalization of drugs, and liberal groups who think by disarming the public they'll make America a safer place.

Activist Christians have had enough, and they're willing to use the democratic process laid down by our founding fathers to thwart the religious left's social redefinition of America.

It's Christian traditional values that made America great, and it's the religious left that is contributing to society's slide into the pagan abyss. Fazio's characterization of the religious right as a "radical and intolerant" fringe force leaves you wondering who is, in fact, intolerant and the bigot. Fearmongering by Clinton and his disciples is clearly a sign that they have begun to panic.

The religious left's call for tolerance by the religious right is somewhat virtuous, but tolerance is also the immediate neighbor of apathy and weakness. It seems that Clinton's desire for tolerance is a polite way of saying "religion is okay so long as it's practiced in the church and home but don't let it interfere with our redefining of America values."

The religious left would do well to remember that Americans still look to their faith as a compass in leading their daily lives. Noted French statesman Alexis de Tocqueville understood the need for religion in society when he penned the following:

> *Freedom sees religion as the companion of its struggles and triumphs, the cradle of its infancy, and the divine source of its rights. Religion is considered as the guardian of mores, and mores regarded as the guarantee of the laws and pledge for the maintenance of freedom itself.*

It's my bet that 137 million Christians will give Bill Clinton and Democrats from the religious left one heck of a wake-up call in the 1994 and 1996 elections.

10 / The Economy

Everybody wants prosperity. The question is how best to achieve it. Liberals believe that an unfettered market creates vast inequalities and that unregulated business results in dangerous work conditions, unsafe products, and low wages for workers. Conservatives believe that government attempts to control the economy or regulate business inhibit economic growth and wind up hurting everyone.

One of the pressing issues facing our economy is the future of organized labor. Are labor unions obsolete and corrupt institutions that make us less competitive in the global market? Or is the labor movement one of the proudest achievements of American democracy? Read what we have to say on the subject and then decide for yourself.

Here's a debate we had on the issue of striker replacement—whether a company should have the right to permanently replace striking workers.

STRIKER REPLACEMENT
(DECEMBER 1993)

RIGHT TO WORK
BY BRADLEY O'LEARY

Organized labor claims the so-called striker replacement bill would re-balance the system of collective bargaining in this country. The truth is that there is already balance in the collective bargaining system, and a striker replacement bill would permanently and dramatically tip the scale in the favor of organized labor.

Current law prohibits employers from firing striking employees but does not prohibit them from hiring permanent replacements. The striker replacement bill would be a bonanza for the flagging organized labor movement as it would prohibit employers from hiring permanent replacement workers during a strike. In other words, labor unions could call a strike any time they want and win practically any strike they call. Big labor will have the ability to force any company to "knuckle under" to their demands or be forced to eventually close down operations. Now what the hell is so "balanced" about that!

Organized labor misrepresents the facts. They have made this bill out to be a moral crusade to right the abuses committed by evil, union-busting employers. The truth again, according to a General Accounting Office report, is that in 1989 only 3 percent of striking workers were permanently replaced. Yet the bill's sponsor, Senator "What Do I Know About the Average Guy" Ted Kennedy is treating this bill with the utmost urgency.

This bill stinks! Not content to smack small and large businesses alike with new taxes and mandated health care coverage, Bill Clinton and his band of liberals in Congress are trying to deal the knockout punch to business by forcing them to accede to practically any and all labor demands.

Congress should refer to this bill by its real name: "The Help Organized Labor off Its Knees Act." Passage of this bill would put all the power in the hands of union bosses. Labor officials will be able to blackmail employers into signing contracts forcing workers to pay union dues. Obviously this bill isn't about restoring balance—it's about replenishing dwindling union membership at a potential cost of jobs to non-union workers.

President Clinton has promised to sign the bill if it reaches his desk, and in doing so he would reverse fifty-five years of U.S. labor policy. Our "fairness" president would be well-served not to tinker with labor policy.

Currently, unions are free to strike, companies are free to hire workers, and individuals are free to work, and nothing could be more fair or more balanced than that. Let's hope it stays that way.

RIGHT TO STRIKE
BY VICTOR KAMBER

Can Senate Republicans—who plan to filibuster the Workplace Fairness Act—offer any coherent explanation of the difference between being "permanently replaced" and being fired for exercising the right to strike?

I haven't heard one yet.

Are they prepared to explain to former striking Eastern Airlines and Greyhound workers that what happened to them was something other than being fired?

Let's face it—allowing workers who strike to be "permanently replaced" when firing striking workers is illegal and is a semantic sham more appropriate to George Orwell's (or, come to think of it, Ronald Reagan's) *1984* than to 1993.

There's a good reason why the National Labor Relations Act bans the firing of striking workers—because when any employee loses his or her job for going out on strike, all workers lose the right to strike. And without that right, collective bargaining becomes a rigged baseball game where Nolan Ryan throws every pitch for management, and one strike and you're out.

With collective bargaining thus undermined, it's no coincidence that the American standard of living— once the highest on the planet—has been in a free fall ever since Reagan gave management a green light to "permanently replace" strikers. Indeed, real weekly wages have dropped nearly 6 percent over the last decade. And it's no coincidence that labor-management relations have gotten more acrimonious as employers like Frank Lorenzo actually instigated strikes just to get rid of their workers and bust their unions.

Passage of the Workplace Fairness Act, which bans the "permanent replacement" of strikers, would remedy many of these problems. It would create a more level playing field between labor and management. This would foster greater cooperation because both sides would have something to lose under a strike and everything to gain from a solid agreement. Remember that even if workers couldn't lose their jobs from striking, they would still lose pay, while having to keep up the mortgage payments and feed the family. And while management couldn't "permanently replace" strikers, they could hire scabs to temporarily keep production going. You're not going to start seeing picket lines on every corner or the sky falling as management Chicken Littles would have you believe.

Greater cooperation on an equal basis will improve U.S. competitiveness. All of our major competitors, including Japan and Germany, ban the "permanent replacement" of strikers. And they have been running circles around us in the global marketplace.

Further, the level playing field created by this bill

will allow unions to negotiate better contracts and start bringing the American standard of living back to the top of the heap where it belongs.

It's time to obliterate Republican gridlock in the Senate, where every measure advancing our nation into the twenty-first century is held hostage by an obstructionist minority. I can think of no better gridlock-busting bill than the Workplace Fairness Act.

• • •

Should the minimum wage be raised? Liberals think it should so that anyone working a 40-hour week is lifted above the poverty line. Conservatives argue that unskilled workers and those just entering the job market are precisely the victims of a higher minimum wage, because they're the first to get fired or not even hired in the first place if a company cannot afford to pay the higher minimum wage.

This is an issue that never goes away, and even though we wrote these columns some time ago, the arguments are still relevant today.

RAISING THE MINIMUM WAGE
(APRIL 1987)

RAISE THE MINIMUM WAGE
BY VICTOR KAMBER

"If a free society cannot help the many who are poor," John Kennedy said in his inaugural address, "it cannot save the few who are rich." The minimum wage was enacted to help the poor climb out of poverty and to save the rich from their own greed.

We have the richest society in the world, and the world's largest market for goods and services. But if the working poor of our nation don't earn enough money to buy the goods and services they produce, how can the rich expect to stay in business?

The goal of the minimum wage when it was first enacted in 1938 was to provide enough to keep a family of three out of poverty. It was also supposed to set a standard equal to roughly half of the average wage for non-supervisory private workers such as secretaries, operators, guards, and janitors.

Today, it does neither.

After maintaining a level of roughly half the average wage for more than forty years, the minimum wage has dropped off dramatically since it was frozen in 1981. According to the George Washington University Center for Policy Studies, it is now just 38.3 percent of the average wage.

And the current minimum wage ($6,968 annually for a full-time earner) is nearly $1,800 less than the 1986 poverty threshold of $8,741 for a family of three.

Led by the Chamber of Commerce, profit-hungry opponents of raising the minimum wage claim that raising wages will force employers to cut jobs. But this is a smokescreen. They are not so much concerned about jobs as they are about profits.

Their real goal is to eliminate the minimum wage altogether. Failing that, they want to render it obsolete by continuing to freeze it.

This is where the rich need to be saved from their own greed.

As any Reagan administration devotee will tell you, there have been many new jobs created during his term in office. But nearly 60 percent of the new jobs created pay less than $7,000 a year—about the minimum wage for a full-time worker.

If jobs tied to the minimum wage are among the fastest growing jobs, freezing the minimum wage will serve over the long haul to lower our nation's standard of living.

Opponents will tell you that those earning the minimum wage are part-time workers or spouses supplementing the principal wage earner's income. Much more typical, however, is the divorced mother of three.

Exemptions in the law allow employers to pay below the minimum wage to workers who earn tip income and to handicapped employees. Workers in small businesses (with annual gross revenue under $362,500) are also not entitled to the minimum wage. This is significant since small business is responsible for creating about two-thirds of all new jobs over the last ten years.

But of the workers who earn the minimum wage, approximately one-fourth were heads of households in 1981 (the most recent year for which figures are available). The majority of those are women.

And nearly 40 percent of minimum wage earners are between the ages of 25 and 64—precisely the group that provides the backbone of our economy.

These are not kids trying to pick up some extra cash for weekends at the movies or a new car. And these are not women working for "pin money," as President Reagan so callously likes to maintain.

They are hard-working Americans—many of whom are eligible for welfare because their wages are so low. And they deserve a living wage that allows them to provide shelter, food, and clothing for their families with dignity.

LOWER THE MINIMUM WAGE
BY BRADLEY O'LEARY

The campaign by Ted Kennedy and the AFL-CIO to raise the minimum wage to $4.61 an hour is deceptive and dangerous. Their campaign will result in increasing unemployment and will bring back inflation, making it harder to sell American goods in foreign markets.

The real goal of Kennedy and the AFL-CIO is to increase production costs and make it easier for union workers earning just above the minimum wage to press for higher wages.

Most economists believe a wage increase would put 400,000 to 1.5 million Americans out of work.

Indeed, in 1975, when we raised the minimum wage, 8.3 percent of all low-wage jobs were eliminated and 1.5 million people were forced out of work in a three-year period.

When America froze the minimum wage in 1981, 63.3 percent of our adult population was employed. Today, 68.7 percent is employed.

Organized labor is only out to regain its political clout and do to Americans what powerful unions have done to our trading partners in Japan and Europe over the last few years.

With powerful trade and labor unions in Japan and Europe winning the legislative battle to increase wages and social benefits, we have seen a major decline in consumer demand among those countries.

In 1981, 65.3 percent of Europe's adult population was employed. Today 57.9 percent is employed.

During that same time America created 11.2 million jobs—only 230,000 of these in the minimum wage area. Our overall employment declined by 28 percent.

In Japan during that period, unemployment rose 17 percent; in Europe, 20 percent.

In these countries powerful organized labor unions have moved Japanese and European governments into a semi-welfare state environment with high taxes, increased early-retirement benefits and a lack of small-business, free-enterprise incentive.

We might consider that we aren't losing the trade war only because of unfair trade practices. We are losing because so many consumers in Japan and Europe are in the welfare line, out of work; while 11 million more Americans are at the stores increasing the demand for American products as well as foreign products. In Europe and Japan demand decreased for both their products and ours.

Under President Carter, imports were 9.4 percent of our gross national product. Under Reagan, it has been reduced—that's right, reduced—to 8.7 percent.

America's exports under Carter were 7.9 percent, under Reagan, 5.2 percent—not because of unfair trade competition, but because so many consumers overseas can't find jobs to earn the money to buy our products.

Our trading partners need to do what we did—cut taxes and reduce welfare. When we did it we released the creativity of the American worker to make America great again.

And we are not finished. Japan, Europe, and the rest of the world cannot compete with American technology, know-how and incentives for the little guy to find his American dream by going into business for himself.

We need to keep the minimum wage at $3.35 and even cut it to $2.50 for youth and summer youth workers.

If we lowered the minimum wage for entry-level jobs that provide young and unskilled workers with their only chance to learn, we would create 400,000 new jobs this year alone.

Over 400,000 young people would be working—not sitting around streets, driven by poverty to think about self-fulfillment through drug abuse or economic independence from a life of crime.

Let's not forget that we raised the minimum wage just before Jimmy Carter came to office and that inflation, interest rates, and unemployment were the result of four years of Jimmy Carter, Teddy Kennedy, the AFL-CIO, and the Democratic-controlled Senate and House.

11 / Health Care

Health care is both an economic and a social issue. And while the Clinton health care plan of 1994 was shot down, don't think for a moment that this debate is over.

Liberals believe that health care coverage should be a right, not a privilege—and while liberals disagree over whether health care should be provided through private insurance or a government run "single payer" system like Canada's, they do agree that government should guarantee coverage for everyone. Conservatives believe that a massive health care bureaucracy would inevitably result from such government action, only raising the cost of medical care and make it less available to everyone.

Here's how we weighed in on the issue during the debate over Clinton's proposal.

HEALTH CARE (SPRING 1994)

THE HEALTH CARE CRISIS
BY VICTOR KAMBER

Despite the claims of Senator Bob Dole, other top Republicans, and their special interest benefactors, we *do* have a health care crisis in this country. When 37 million Americans are uninsured and 58 million have no health insurance for some time each year, no other word applies.

That is why the number one goal of health care reform must be to guarantee comprehensive coverage for *all* Americans.

And that is the number one reason why Congress should enact President Clinton's health care reform program.

Not one of the Republican and conservative alternative plans does this—not Cooper, Chafee, Gramm, Nickels or Michel. To not provide universal coverage is akin to rearranging the deck chairs on the *Titanic*. If you are not given the security of knowing your health care coverage can never be taken away, you still risk losing everything—even your life—to the health care iceberg.

The Clinton plan's method of universal coverage— employer mandates combined with subsidies for small businesses and for lower-income individuals who are self-employed or unemployed—has particular merit. It builds on the present system of employer-provided coverage, while eliminating cost-shifting —the extra premium insured people pay to cover the medical costs of the uninsured. It also ends the unfair cost advantage gained by irresponsible employers that effectively pass their employees' health care buck to their competitors.

Contrary to GOP mythmaking and fearmongering, health care costs will go *down* for most employers under the Clinton bill. Employee health premiums will be capped at 7.9 percent of payroll—many corporations spend more than twice that today. Small, low-wage businesses may pay as little as 3.5 percent of payroll for health care. Republican and conservative plans contain no such caps.

The Clinton plan stands head and shoulders above the field in all other key aspects of health care reform:

- It provides concrete cost controls by limiting the amount insurance companies can raise annual premiums—not one alternative plan does this.

- It *increases* patient choice because all Americans will pick from at least three health plans, including a traditional fee-for-service plan with complete doctor choice—the GOP/conservative plans maintain or speed up the current trend of funneling people into HMOs.

- It preserves quality by guaranteeing a comprehensive benefits package to every American as good or better than that offered by most large corporations—the GOP/conservative plans fail to spell out a minimum benefits package.

It's time for Republicans to get their heads out of the sand and acknowledge the severity of our health care crisis. It's time for Republicans to stop flacking for the special interests and start listening to the American people. And it's time for Republicans to put aside partisanship and work to enact the only plan to achieve true health care reform, President Clinton's Health Security Act.

WHAT HEALTH CARE CRISIS?
BY BRADLEY O'LEARY

When I listen to Bill and Hillary pitch their health care plan, the old adage, "you don't get something for nothing" comes to mind. The Clinton health care plan will definitely provide you with less health care, send the federal deficit soaring, perhaps cost you your job, and, in the extreme, your life—all in the name of "universal coverage."

Congressional Republicans and most of the nation's governors are absolutely right for claiming there is no crisis in health care, and most Americans would appear to agree with them. A *Time*/CNN poll showed that 51 percent of Americans believe no crisis exists, 67 percent thought the cost of health care was too high, and only 27 percent felt that coverage was a problem. Did you get that, Bill? The problem with America's health care system is that it costs too much. It's the Cost, Stupid!

The only "crisis" in health care that might exist is the one that would be created by Bill Clinton's socialized prescription for America. Big government does not run large programs effectively or efficiently. Bill and Hillary Clinton's proposal is oriented in the wrong direction. Rather than scrap the best health care system in the world in the name of "universal coverage" we should look at ways to get coverage for those 37 million who go at some point in time during the year without insurance, and work at reducing costs. If we want expanded health care coverage for the 13.5 million of those 37.5 million that are on welfare but not covered by Medicaid then we should provide for them in the welfare reform bill. If we want to cover the 4.3 million of those 37 million that are under correctional supervision, then let's provide for them in the next omnibus crime bill. We should not worry about the many millions of illegal immigrants who are counted in that 37 million. Most of those illegal immigrants do not pay taxes but manage to enjoy federal benefits in any event.

We need only look at the Canadian health care system to see that big government is not the answer. They have one-tenth of our population and a fraction of the number of major urban areas and yet waits of three to six months are common for patients awaiting needed surgery. Rationed care, long waits, and declining numbers of doctors are all symptoms of a Canadian system suffering from the wrong prescription.

Republicans want to adopt market-oriented reforms for our health care system. Some of the GOP proposals include: the establishment of Medical Savings Accounts (MSAs) that would work much like IRAs; tax credits for those who cannot afford coverage; requiring insurance companies to rate and cover everyone; and tax credits for those with higher premiums due to serious illness.

Bill and Hillary Clinton's proposal isn't even a noble idea. The big-government approach to health care isn't about universal coverage—it's about empowering bureaucrats and the Democrats in Congress who oversee them. The Republican proposals address the problem and promise to keep big government and even bigger deficits out of our lives.

• • •

Several months later, Clinton's proposal was in trouble, and we considered the issue again.

HEALTH CARE (OCTOBER 1994)

DEAD ON ARRIVAL
BY BRADLEY O'LEARY

The body of President Clinton's health care plan is barely cold, having flatlined while on the operating room table, and what do we see? Doctor Mitchell and Doctor Gephardt desperately using their voodoo "magic" to revive this corpse. It does sound morbid but what the Democrats are offering America is nothing more than major portions of the Clinton health care plan stitched together in the hope that Americans won't recognize it for what it really is. To most Americans, what Mitchell and Gephardt are offering is pretty ugly. Somebody forgot to tell Bill and Hillary's medicine men on the Hill that America wants no part of employer mandates or any plan calling for government-run health care. I guess the notion of government "bureausurgeons" who pick at your wallet rather than your brain just plain scares the "bejabbers" out of most people!

Americans may be fuzzy about what specifically they want included in health care legislation, but they are absolute in what they don't want. An ABC News poll conducted in July showed that 42 percent of Americans approve of the Clinton health care plan while *49 percent disapprove* and another 8 percent had no opinion. That same poll showed that 52 percent of Americans felt holding down cost was most important. Only 43 percent felt that guaranteeing health insurance was the more important goal for health care. Are any of these national moods driving health care? Obviously not. In fact, the only thing driving health care reform is political expediency, selfishness and arrogance. The Clintons, Mitchell, and Gephardt have yet to adequately answer a number of questions:

- Why must we take private health insurance away from 85 percent of Americans and substitute it with a trillion dollar government plan (if that's even the true cost) that covers an additional 10 percent of Americans?

- Why will members of Congress and their staffs still be exempt from any of the Democratic proposals?

- Why are we trying to scrap the best health care system in the world in favor of one run by the same sort of folks who administer Social Security and welfare and deliver the mail?

- Why the rush?

The last question is probably the most offensive. There is nothing more than politics driving this issue and what's worse are its desperation politics aimed at saving the hide of the Democratic Party. America should refer to the Clinton, Mitchell, and Gephardt bills as the "Political Security Act." And, if any of those plans succeed, can America sue for legislative malpractice?

The Clinton, Mitchell, and Gephardt plans all share signs of terminal illness: employer mandates, new taxes, new entitlements, rationed health care, and price controls. America doesn't need that kind of quackery, gents, and it certainly should be wary of a plan with unspecified costs that goes into effect after many current leaders have long retired. So what do Mitchell and Gephardt care? They'll still be exempt from any such plan no matter what happens.

It's time for Democratic leaders to work with Republicans who have solid proposals for reforming health care. Those proposals call for medical savings accounts, no new taxes and no mandates; and, best of all, we get to keep our first-rate health care system.

Killing Health Care Reform
By Victor Kamber

Throughout American history, every fight by Democrats to make our society more humane and decent

by meeting the needs of middle-class, working families has been opposed by a reactionary, narrow-
minded, elitist Republican Party. Every time, history
has proven the Democrats right and the GOP wrong.

According to the Republican Party at the time
these proposals were debated, Social Security and
unemployment insurance would make workers indo-
lent and grass grow on the streets. Medicare and
Medicaid would lead to socialized medicine. Civil
rights legislation would destroy the American way of
life.

History has proven these programs and advance-
ments so successful that today, you won't hear a single Republican bad-mouthing them, at least
on-the-record.

So it is with health care reform.

If legislation guaranteeing every American health
insurance that can never be taken away had
passed this session, ten and twenty years from today,
politicians of both parties would ask how we ever
managed without it. It would be a political sacred
cow.

But with such legislation apparently killed off by
Newt Gingrich, Bob Dole, Phil Gramm, and a group
of conservative Democrats who have been bought
lock, stock and barrel by the insurance industry, this is
a sad day in American history. Voters will look back
on this as the day America decided it could no
longer afford to be great, as the day politicians sided
with the special interest against working families.

That's what this was all about.

Every Republican member of Congress should be
forced to explain to the voters why he or she is enti-
tled to first rate health care coverage (at taxpayer
expense, no less), but families have no such right.

Every Republican in Congress should be forced to

explain to the voters why he or she chose obstructionism, political gamesmanship and gridlock over solving the life and death problems facing the American people.

Every Republican in Congress should be forced to explain why businesses should have the right to force other employers, consumers and taxpayers to pay for the medical care of their employees, and why insurance companies should have the right to screw over their customers.

Every Republican in Congress should be forced to meet with the 37 million Americans who have no health insurance and explain why he or she voted for the special interests and against them.

If the GOP can explain this away with transparent, misleading and cynical rhetoric about "big government" and "socialized medicine," then maybe America's voters don't deserve to have a right to health insurance.

But if the voters are as smart as I think they are, they will take one look at what the Republicans did to health care reform and kick out the party of big-money sleaze, electing instead Democratic candidates committed to improving the quality of life for middle-class American families.

12 / Crime

Both conservatives and liberals agree that crime is an immense problem, and we have to take serious measures to control it. But that's where the agreement ends.

Liberals seek to alleviate the root causes of crime while conservatives want to build more prisons and incarcerate more criminals. Conservatives are more interested in punishment, while liberals make prevention the high priority.

One of the more revealing debates is how liberals and conservatives would treat violent juvenile criminals. Here's how we come down on this controversial issue.

JUVENILE JUSTICE (MAY 1994)

PREVENTION FIRST
BY VICTOR KAMBER

Skyrocketing juvenile crime—and its increasingly barbaric nature—is appalling. But frying thirteen year-olds in the electric chair is no less barbaric. Indeed, trying minors as adults won't stop this crime wave, because teenage murderers don't think about the consequences of their actions. It's no deterrent.

So the right-wingers essentially say, "Let them kill and after they do we'll give them life sentences or capital punishment." I say, "Let's stop teenagers from killing in the first place." How do we do this? I see two approaches.

First, get handguns out of their hands. Kids today find it easier to buy a Beretta than to buy a pack of Bazooka bubble gum at the corner grocery store. This is an outrage.

We must give long-term jail sentences to any adult who sells a handgun or ammunition to a minor; make it illegal for any minor to possess a handgun; and hold handgun and ammunition manufacturers and dealers liable for the deaths and injuries their products cause.

Second, we must reemphasize treatment. Sure, some teenagers are psychopaths who cannot be rehabilitated. But most are still growing and capable of change under the right circumstances. How can we, as a society, just give up on a thirteen year-old—even one who has committed the most heinous acts?

Giving up means sending them to jail—taxpayer-funded crime universities that give young offenders the opportunity to learn the tricks of the trade from their new role models: adult murderers and rapists.

In Massachusetts, aggressive treatment programs in juvenile facilities have significantly reduced re-arrest rates. Violent offenders are taught new skills in resolving conflict and dealing with anger that enable them to avoid violence—and they are taught how to think about the consequences of their actions *before* doing something. These programs also give teenage offenders positive role models—something missing from their lives.

Treatment is also essential because so many juvenile crimes are the result of drug and alcohol abuse. Get them off drugs, and they'll get off the cycle of violence.

We have been spending 94 percent of our anti-crime dollars on punishment and only 6 percent on prevention—all the while teenage crime continues to soar. This horrific trend will only be reversed when we give those who can be saved the skills to start a new life, rather than condemning them to a life of crime, a life on the taxpayer dole in our prisons, or no life at all.

DO THE CRIME, SERVE THE TIME
BY BRADLEY O'LEARY

Society has a primary duty to punish juvenile offenders, not to rehabilitate them.

The punishment of boot camp, life imprisonment, or execution should fit the viciousness of the crime, not the age of the violent offender. As a society, we cannot show any sympathy for, or accept any excuses from, the young thugs, perverts, and psychopaths who are destroying our schools and neighborhoods.

Thousands of young violent offenders have no moral compass and no fear of punishment. Worst of all, many have no sense of right and wrong. The statistics are shocking and grim. According to Uniform Crime Reports for the United States, in 1992, 2,829 juveniles were arrested for murder, 5,369 for forcible rape, 40,434 for robbery, and 63,777 for aggravated assault. The National Crime Victimization Survey conducted a few years ago by the Justice Department estimated that some 430,000 children had been the victims of rape, robbery, or assault at school. These are the children we must protect—not those who lack religious beliefs, eat the wrong diet, were abused by family members, or were driven to violence by television or music. Those are not valid reasons for our citizens to live in perpetual fear of evil kids and violent juvenile offenders.

What can we do? Curfews for young people in shopping malls and other public areas should be instituted. And all the estimated 270,000 children who bring a gun or a knife to school each day should be sent to boot camp for six months. Any juvenile who uses a deadly weapon in committing a crime should be given a mandatory one-year prison sentence.

Juveniles arrested for crimes like rape and murder should not be let off by too-lenient courts or age-mandated early-release programs. They should serve time like adults and even face the prospect of society's ultimate solution for violent offenders—no matter what their age. Juveniles fourteen or older must be tried as adults for violent crimes involving rape, murder, armed robbery, and aggravated assault.

The first lesson that should be taught in school is: you do the crime, you serve the time. Parents, teachers, and society as a whole will not enjoy peace of mind until our schools and streets are free of violent juveniles.

• • •

This difference of approach between liberals and conservatives is starkest in the debate over the death penalty. Most liberals oppose the death penalty as cruel and unusual punishment. Most conservatives favor the death penalty as a deterrent, or at least just retribution.

Here's what we think about capital punishment.

THE DEATH PENALTY (JUNE 1990)

THE DEATH PENALTY WORKS—LET'S USE IT
BY BRADLEY O'LEARY

Every year 20,000 Americans are murdered. And every year, the vast majority of these murders are drug-related, particularly in big cities. A fact of life in our criminal justice system is that less than 2 percent of the murderers in this country are convicted; the rest find themselves sheltered by a judicial system that can no longer protect the victims of crime.

Offenders know that for even the most heinous crimes, if caught and sentenced to "life imprisonment," chances are they will be out on the streets within a few years. Life imprisonment is a liberal scam.

The only way we can guarantee justice to the poor—who are the principal victims of crime—and protect middle-class America, is to administer the death penalty to these vicious criminals.

Traditionally, the American public has overwhelmingly been behind the concept of capital punishment. In the 1920s, after a rash of kidnapping-for-ransoms (culminating in the Lindbergh case) the U.S. strictly enforced the death penalty. Today, kidnapping is almost unheard of. The time has come for us to demand the same federal penalty for small and big time drug dealers who are turning the U.S.'s playgrounds into war zones.

The citizens of this country must exercise their vote and demand that both federal and state governments pass and enforce laws that protect our communities from these criminals. The American public long ago gave up the notion that all criminals can be rehabilitated, and a majority have consistently supported the death penalty since at least 1936.

Patrick Purdy, who murdered twelve children on a playground in Stockton, California, was out of jail because the criminal justice system let him plea bargain five felony convictions. This is just one famous example of a tragedy caused by the politicians' concept of "rehabilitation."

The liberal politicians will tell you that Purdy was a victim of society. In reality, those choosing to delay justice at the expense of our children and our safety will find themselves voted out of office by the growing constituency of victims.

Americans are living in fear and frustration because of a criminal justice system that is constantly failing. They are paying the price for a system that relies too heavily on lenient judges and early parole.

The death penalty is only one facet of a complex answer to the drug and crime problem. Overhauling the criminal justice system so that criminals can't get out on the streets before the victim can get out of the hospital and limiting the number of times a criminal can plea bargain in a five-year period are imperative reforms.

Together with increased jail space, tougher sentencing, and speedy trials, which bring criminals to justice before they are eligible for Social Security, the death penalty needs to be used to clean up our streets, to protect our children, and to stop the rampant epidemic of crime.

THE DEATH PENALTY IS A CRIME
BY VICTOR KAMBER

And I thought civilization had advanced beyond "An eye for an eye, a tooth for a tooth."

Well, this antiquated notion was shattered by the grisly ad campaigns of former Texas Governor Mark White (D) and Florida Governor Bob Martinez (R) in 1990. White walked by larger-than-life mug shots of people executed in Texas and bragged about how he had them killed. Martinez showed video-tape footage of serial killer Ted Bundy and boasted of frying him in the electric chair.

In all my years in politics, I've never felt sicker to my stomach.

Politics can be a force for good when leaders try to touch the best instincts that are within us. But it can do great damage when gutless candidates exploit our worst fears.

Of course, the thousands of death penalty proponents running for office—even those who "don't believe in it, but are just carrying out the law"—say it's a matter of survival. When polls show 80 percent backing the death penalty, any politician would be suicidal to oppose it.

Well, these politicians aren't just spineless—they're not even reading the polls carefully. If they did, they'd find out most voters, when presented with the alternative of life imprisonment without parole, prefer that option.

Politics aside, the death penalty is a crime, because:

1) It's murder. Government sets the moral tone for society. When government decides certain circumstances warrant the premeditated taking of a human life, it creates a climate where criminals feel even more justified making similar judgments.

2) It's discriminatory. Blacks convicted of murder are more likely to be sentenced to death than whites. When the victim is white, the death penalty is more likely to be imposed, as well. The death penalty's scales of justice are disgracefully unbalanced.

3) It's cruel and unusual. Without getting into the gruesome details here, suffice it to say that even lethal injection—supposedly the most "humane" form of murder—inflicts horrible cruelty on its victims.

4) It's no deterrent. There are two ways people kill others. Either they plan the murder in advance, at the same time taking steps not to get caught. Or, they kill in a spontaneous rage, without stopping to think about the consequences of their actions. Gun control would have an infinitely greater deterrent value.

5) It's more expensive than life imprisonment. It costs Florida $3.2 million, on average, to impose the death penalty, due to the extensive—and well-justified—appeals process. Life imprisonment saves taxpayer dollars.

6) It kills innocent people. Our legal system may be the world's best, but it makes mistakes. Wrongly jailed prisoners can be freed when new evidence comes to light. But modern technology has yet to devise a way to bring back the dead.

It's time our elected officials showed some courage, decency, and, yes, even morality—and ended this sordid chapter in our nation's history.

13 / National Defense

The disagreements between liberals and conservatives on the issue of national defense are profound and deeply rooted in their opposing philosophies. Conservatives believe in a strong and active defense. Liberals are often suspicious of military adventures and prefer making peace rather than waging war. In the trade-off between guns and butter (defense and welfare programs), conservatives would rather have guns, while liberals prefer butter.

One of the first controversies in the beginning of the Clinton presidency was the issue of whether gays and lesbians should be allowed to serve in the military. This debate brings the differing outlooks that liberals and conservatives have on sexual orientation to bear on important considerations of national defense.

Should gays be allowed to openly serve in the military? Do they threaten morale? Was Clinton right in compromising, or did he cave in to the special interests?

GAYS IN THE MILITARY (JULY 1993)

END THE BIGOTRY

BY VICTOR KAMBER

> Government governs best when it governs least—and stays out of the impossible task of legislating morality. But legislating someone's version of morality is exactly what we do by perpetuating discrimination against gays....You don't need to be `straight' to fight and die for your country. You just need to shoot straight.
>
> — Barry Goldwater, *The Washington Post*

I never thought the day would come when I would quote Mr. "Extremism in the defense of liberty is no vice" to talk sense into my conservative colleague, but here it is.

The U.S. military's function is to defend our nation and the values for which we stand: freedom, liberty, and tolerance. Its purpose is not to be a giant irony—or worse, a blot on our nation—by violating these values through a policy that states "homosexuality is incompatible with military service."

That policy is one big lie. Gays have fought for our country with the same heroism as straights and will continue to do so.

The ultimate refutation of this policy comes from Israel, which has perhaps the world's most respected, effective, and fierce fighting force, and, unlike the U.S., depends upon the military for its very survival. Since its founding forty-five years ago, the Israeli military has permitted gays to serve, and they have done so honorably through four full-scale wars, hundreds of smaller skirmishes, and a constant state of alert.

According to a recent General Accounting Office report commissioned by Senator John Warner (R-VA), who is no supporter of gays in the military, "Israeli officials said that homosexuals have performed as well as heterosexuals and have served successfully in all branches of the military since 1948....*Homosexuals... have not hurt their units' morale, cohesion, readiness, or capability* (italics added), based on the experiences of military officials."

Now if that's not enough to convince homophobics like Senator Sam Nunn (D-GA), who is too chicken to run for president and too narcissistic to stop acting out his presidential fantasies on this issue, consider these other facts:

- We are wasting a whopping *$500 million* investigating and discharging gay servicemembers not because of their conduct but because of who they are.

- Military leaders and people with Nunn's mindset raised the same red herrings when blacks and women were integrated into the military. They were proven wrong then, just as they will be proven wrong now.

- The notion that our troops will start shooting at one another if gays serve is equally ludicrous. A soldier's job is to follow orders; if he violates any order—whether by attacking gays or doing something else—he doesn't belong in the military. Canada's experience confirms this. As *The Washington Post* reported, "The nine months since (gays were allowed to join Canada's military) have been virtually casualty-free. No resignations, violence or harassment have been reported....Straight soldiers...say they have accepted the new regime."

It's time to cut through the bigotry, stereotyping, and myth-making and accept reality—lifting the ban on gays in the military will not hurt readiness or unit cohesion in the least. It will save money and give all Americans willing and able to serve the opportunity to do so. Most important, it will enable the military to embrace the values it is charged with defending.

CAVING IN TO THE GAYS
BY BRADLEY O'LEARY

Bill Clinton campaigned on a pledge to close the Oval Office door to special interests. Ironically, not one month into his presidency, Clinton caved in to demands from the largest special interest group that helped elect him president. That group, the gay rights lobby, collected over $5 million on behalf of Bill Clinton, and that sum accounts for nearly one-fifth of the total amount raised by the Clinton campaign in 1992.

President Clinton's goal is to force you and me to endorse a lifestyle—a gay lifestyle—of one of his special interest groups. Not only does he want civilians to endorse the gay lifestyle, but he also wants to force this lifestyle on our nation's military personnel. What really galls me is that Bill Clinton has a disdain for the military establishment, and we still don't know the truth about what he did to avoid military service and we know he did a lot.

He has not one idea of what the military life of the average enlistee is like. He's never had to "hot bunk" on a submarine (where two or three sailors take turns sleeping in the same bunk). He's never experienced the primitive living conditions to which our military forces are sometimes subjected.

The president's plan for "softening" the gay ban is not based on real-world experience. It's more likely that the president's proposal was developed in the vacuum of his Ivy League education. Bill Clinton and Hillary Rodham Clinton probably developed their sense of fairness for gays in the military while dining one night on salmon and good wine.

President Clinton appears to be more concerned with tearing down the greatest fighting force in the world than maintaining it. His proposal to end the gay ban is at odds with his constitutional responsibility to ensure that our armed forces are ready to fight. Clinton fails to understand that the issue is not about gay individuals but about unit cohesion. Differences

between each member of our fighting forces are min-
imized—not enhanced—so that troops function as a
team. Clinton does not comprehend the military's
lifestyle of forced association. As General Colin Powell
pointed out on ABC's *Nightline:* "To introduce a group
of individuals who...favor a homosexual lifestyle, and
put them in with heterosexuals who would prefer not
to have somebody of the same sex find them sexually
attractive...put them in close proximity, ask them to
share the most private of their facilities together—the
bedroom, the barracks, latrines, the showers—I think
that's a very difficult problem to give the military."

President Clinton cannot change the mindsets of
our young heterosexual military men and women
who are troubled by homosexuality. It is their discom-
fort with the notion of homosexuality—not their
homophobia—that would ruin personal bonds and
unit cohesion. Again, the notion of teamwork is lost
on Bill Clinton, and it comes as no surprise given his
track record in office. The president is unable to
weed out myth from fact. It is myth that gays have a
right to serve in our armed forces. Military service is a
privilege. Period. Our military has a responsibility to
put together the best fighting forces it can. Conse-
quently, military service is legally restricted or denied
to Americans who are too fat, too short, too tall, etc.

The threat of AIDS is a very real concern for our
forces and could increase should the gay ban be
lifted. Our fighting forces should not be exposed to
the additional risks of HIV-infected blood. Homosexuals as a group have much higher incidences of AIDS
than heterosexuals. Why should we unnecessarily
expose our troops to additional risks for the sake of
gay rights?

The president should listen to his highly intelligent
and highly decorated senior officers when they say

his proposal stinks. Just look at the findings from a recent survey conducted by the House Republican Research Committee. The vast majority of the 621 senior military officers who responded thought that allowing gays to serve in the military was a bad idea. Ninety-seven percent of them also think that allowing gays to serve in the military will make future young men and women less likely to join our volunteer military. Hell, even Democratic Senator Sam Nunn thinks the idea stinks!

Bill Clinton has opted to listen to the cadre of individuals, who, like himself, share a social revisionist agenda. Our president has made the first priority of his administration to deliver for a special interest group that delivered for him in the campaign. His goal is to thrust a lifestyle upon the heterosexual civilian and military population that largely refuses to accept that lifestyle as equivalent to their own.

• • •

During the 1980s, the debate over aid to the Nicaraguan Contras divided conservatives and liberals along clear party lines. Liberals felt that American support of the Contras was illegal and immoral, and could possibly lead into direct military involvement. Conservatives wanted to get the communist Sandinistas out of the Nicaraguan government.

Now that the cold war has frozen over and the international conflicts no longer fall into predictable spheres of Communism versus the Free World many national defense issues are not so clear as the debate over the Contras. But revisiting this controversy clearly delineates the liberal and conservative positions on national defense during that period.

CONTRA AID (MARCH 1987)

THE SANDINISTA CONSPIRACY

BY BRADLEY O'LEARY

Imagine a day when refugees come pouring across our border into Texas and California. Imagine a million or two coming into New Mexico, with its population of one million, and millions more coming into Arizona and Nevada.

Anyone who travels through Mexico can see it is a nation on the verge of revolution, fueled by massive poverty and chaotic economic instability, worsened by an oil crisis.

Mexicans pour across our border even today while there is no revolution. How many more would come if a Castro or Sandinista type government were to take control, eliminating any freedom they may still have?

All the seeds are there: massive corruption; oppression of the poor; a ruling class intent on profits and suppressing reform. These, combined with their economic state, create a country primed to be plowed by any garden variety Communist dictator.

When we think about aid to the Contras we must remember that the Sandinista goal, after achieving insurrection and unrest in El Salvador, Costa Rica, and Honduras, is to encourage that insurrection in Mexico.

In 1979, the Sandinistas began sponsoring guerilla movements, terrorism and other forms of subversion in those countries.

In 1981, though, the first Contra resistance movement against the Sandinistas began gradually drying up the Sandinista arms to El Salvador.

This was in part because the Contras were able to capture convoys destined for El Salvador, and partly because the Sandinistas, faced with armed conflict, could no longer afford to donate manpower, logistics and arms needed to defend themselves.

If the Democratic leadership in Congress betrays the president and backs out on our commitment to the Contras, it may bring "peace" to Nicaragua, but suppress their only chance for freedom.

If the U.S. denies its commitment to back the Contras, the Sandinistas—faced with a victory no less important than Hitler's in Czechoslovakia—will find adventurous uses for their army. The Nicaraguan army is the biggest and best equipped army in Central America, larger and better equipped than Mexico's army.

I was in Berlin in 1961 and saw the faces of women and children who attempted to cross the border, only to be shot down by freedom-loving revolutionaries.

I was in Vietnam in 1964 and saw the marks of torture on the faces of priests, nuns, ministers, and children whose only crime was to seek to worship the God of their choice.

I went to Pakistan and saw the endless lines of refugee tents that housed 3 million people from an original Afghan population of 16 million. Including the 2 million refugees in Iran, 30 percent of the population fled.

There are currently over a half million refugees in exile from an original Nicaraguan population of 2.8 million. The stability of the Western Hemisphere may depend on support of the Contras.

So when 30 percent, or 24 million, of Mexico's 80 million citizens seek sanctuary and freedom in the United States, we will be faced with closing our borders and returning them to certain death or coping with the most massive influx of refugees the world has ever seen.

The $50 million that we have pledged to give in continued Contra aid is only a drop in the bucket compared to the billions we could be faced with in welfare benefits to a refugee population.

The Soviets do not have an endless supply of funds or military equipment. And they don't have the economic stability to continue to back up the world adventurism they have displayed in Central America, as proven by the fact that we are beginning to see the Russian economic and military withdrawal in areas like Angola and Afghanistan.

If the cost of supporting the Sandinistas becomes too expensive, as it will if the Contras can continue to slow them down, they may find themselves with Soviet aid to defend their borders, but without the money and equipment to underwrite revolutionary campaigns in El Salvador, Honduras, Costa Rica, and Mexico.

JUST SAY NO TO CONTRA AID
BY VICTOR KAMBER

"Contras?" "Freedom fighters?" That's like calling Hitler's SS the "Mouseketeers." President Reagan can call the Nicaraguan rebels what he wants, but I call them terrorists, drug smugglers, mercenaries, and butchers. Not exactly the kind of people I'd like to have over for dinner—let alone have my tax dollars.

Except for a few political front men who handle most of the testifying before Congress, the rebel forces in Nicaragua are made up and led by former supporters and National Guardsmen of deposed Nicaraguan dictator Anastasio Somoza. They were guilty of brutal assassinations, torture, and rape for forty years under Somoza, and they've continued the same bloody tactics in their attempts to over-throw the Sandinista government.

Anyone who looks at their past history and their cur-rent actions can recognize that the rebels aren't so much concerned with political freedom as they are the freedom to use the weapons of their choice.

The Reagan administration has continually attempted to keep quiet the hideous atrocities per-petrated by the rebels. And they have ignored the confessions of Americans Gary Betzner and George Morales that they smuggled cocaine into the U.S. on behalf of the rebels. (Perhaps the president should direct his "Just say 'No' to drugs" campaign to his beloved rebels.)

Even as staunch a critics of the Sandinistas as Catholic Cardinal Obando y Bravo has stated that the Sandinistas have eliminated the government-sponsored torture that characterized the Somoza regime. The problem today, as in the past, lies with the reckless Somoza-inspired military forces—which still form the core of the 10,000–12,000 rebel troops.

It is currently popular among right-wing Republi-cans to point to the bloodshed caused by Commu-nist forces in Southeast Asia after U.S. withdraw from Vietnam and to say that continued U.S. involvement could have prevented it. Why should anyone be against repressive Communist bloodshed in South-east Asia and in favor of its dictatorial counterpart in Central America? Anastasio Somoza led one of the most brutally oppressive regimes in the Western Hemisphere for forty years. Continued aid to the rebels would bring that kind of terror back to power.

But the problem of giving aid to the rebels is not as simple as giving it to the wrong side. It is also the wrong analysis of the situation.

The Sandinista revolution did not start in Moscow. It

did not start in Havana. It started in the small, poverty-stricken country of less than three million people, where more than 70 percent of the wealth was controlled by 1 percent of the population. It started in the country where the vast majority of the people lived without political or economic freedom—but in fear of speaking out against the government.

This country of less than three million is hardly the threatening red menace that President Reagan would like us to imagine. Sixty percent of the economy is in private hands. There are twelve opposition parties, seven of which are represented in the National Assembly. The church, whose leader is one of the strongest critics of the Sandinistas, continues to be one of the strongest institutions in the country. In short, Nicaragua looks much more like a struggling mouse than a fearsome Soviet bear.

Rather than support a band of trigger-happy thugs, the United States would do better to deal with the very real problems of Nicaragua and Central America. We could begin by supporting the peace process promoted by the Latin American nations that make up the Contadora Group, led by Mexico.

Instead of trying to isolate Nicaragua economically, we could attempt to increase its dependency on us—as we have done successfully before. There is no hesitancy to trade with other Communist nations, such as mainland China. Indeed, we have seen a boom in trade with China under Ronald Reagan.

Another step might be to increase economic aid to the region, since the core of the difficulty throughout the region is economics, not politics.

"Contras?" "Freedom fighters?" Call them what you want, but don't give them any of my tax money.

14 / Politics

Politics. Sometimes there's no better word for it. Being political professionals (some would call us political junkies), many of our disagreements are about politics itself. Liberals and conservatives often find themselves divided over such basic political questions as: How should our elections be arranged and financed? Should elected politicians be limited to a number of terms? How can we get more voters registered?

These questions about the nature of the political process itself are interesting not just to political pros, but to every voter. The way we conduct our politics will have a great impact on the way politics affects our lives.

The term limits movement is one of the most powerful (or dangerous) phenomenon in recent political history. Polls show that a majority of Americans want term limits. But would they really solve the problem of entrenched incumbency and political corruption?

TERM LIMITS (NOVEMBER 1990)

TERM LIMITS WOULD BRING NEW ENERGY TO GOVERNMENT
BY BRADLEY O'LEARY

Our forefathers envisioned a citizens' Congress composed of ordinary people, whose strength was in its constantly changing makeup. To foster stability while maintaining close ties to the people, the framers of government set the term of office for the Senate to six years and the House to two.

Politics 133

Today, we see a plethora of stories about how voter participation is down. It is no coincidence that these stories have increased as our political system has moved further from the course set by the original framers.

Today, in many congressional and legislative districts, sons or daughters succeed their parents, as if their seats were inherited in a will.

And today, our leaders are using millions of your tax dollars to send you "constituent mail" that they hope takes the place of personal contact. These mailings, which increase astronomically during election years, are another beam in support of the current Imperial Congress.

Soon, if members of Congress stay in office long enough, they will enjoy millions of dollars in retirement benefits on the taxpayers' tab.

The solution to the imperial, ineffective, and unbelievably overpriced dinosaur called Congress—and to state legislatures, which emulate federal practices—is to set limit terms. Candidates no longer run to serve the people—they run for the security of a lifetime job.

Alan Cranston, a senator for twenty years, is a prime example of the abuses this system creates. He was so petrified of losing his job, he sought to bend the political process by accepting millions of dollars from donors, like Charles Keating, for a tax-deductible foundation designed to register likely Cranston supporters and turn them out to vote.

Rather than inventing meaningful solutions to the budget question, crime, drugs, or the economy, the great majority of the 535 members of Congress are pursuing 535 personal agendas—to get more power, perks and seniority, all of which will help them keep their jobs.

This trend robs government of the creativity and power of new thinking, which served America so well before congressional service was turned into a lifetime occupation. If elected officials cannot accomplish their legislative goals in ten or twelve years, they never should have been elected in the first place.

With the passage of term limitations, voter participation and political involvement would increase, and Americans would have an opportunity to fulfill the framers' dreams by electing citizen legislators with fresh ideas, new energy and a new commitment to solving the U.S.'s problems.

Term Limits: Right Problem, Wrong Solution
By Victor Kamber

The term limitation ballot initiative is a political trojan horse.

It masquerades as a cure-all to democratize our governing bodies and reduce special interest influence. But once inside the castle walls, it will give unelected lobbyists and bureaucrats more power than they could ever have imagined—at the expense of average citizens.

A limit on terms passed in Oklahoma, and it's on the November 6th ballot in California, Colorado, and Missouri. The motivation of initiative proponents is understandable—they're fed up with incumbents and frustrated by their inability to "throw the bums out." They may have the problem right, but the solution is dead wrong.

There is a clear, time-tested remedy already in place for citizens wishing to oust incompetent or wrong-headed public officials: vote for their opponents in the next election. No office-holder is elected for life—each must face the voters at intervals of two, four or six years.

A term limitation prevents citizens from keeping their representatives in office if they're doing a good job. It takes the decision *away* from the very people who should make it—the voters. It's an insult to their intelligence, effectively stating that voters are incapable of chosing their own leaders. It's fundamentally undemocratic.

If incumbents have an unfair advantage in today's elections due to the exhorbitant funds they are able to raise and their staff's functioning as a permanent re-election office, the solution should be obvious: reform campaign finance laws to put challengers on a level playing field.

Limit campaign budgets and establish public financing so non-incumbents can spend the same amount as their opponents. Reduce the number of staff representatives that senators can hire, and limit their responsibilities. But don't prevent good men and women from seeking re-election.

When public officials are limited to eight or twelve years in office, then power will shift to the permanent, unelected bureaucracies entrenched in our state capitals and in Washington, DC. Even worse, special interest lobbyists will have more seniority and more knowledge of the workings of government than the people they're lobbying.

The nation will also be deprived of some of its finest public servants. Many officials—Speakers Tom Foley and Tip O'Neill and the late Representative Claude Pepper (even Republicans like Gerald Ford and Senator Bob Dole), for example, made their greatest contributions after decades in office.

Term limitation supporters are backing the wrong

horse. They should switch to a thoroughbred—campaign finance reform—to accomplish their goals.

• • •

Some apparently parochial political issues can actually have important national implications. Let's take the example of statehood for the District of Columbia. Should the District become the 51st state? Or should it remain under the jurisdiction of the Congress? As you will see, this is an issue that effects all Americans, not just those who live in the nation's capital.

DC STATEHOOD (SEPTEMBER 1992)

GIVE THE DISTRICT A VOICE
BY VICTOR KAMBER

"No taxation without representation" was the battle cry of America's forefathers fighting to free themselves from Colonial rule and determine their own destiny.

Yet the great democracy they founded has a giant blind spot right in its center: the District of Columbia, America's last colony and a place where 608,000 people—more than the population of three other states—are taxed without representation.

It is a crime against democracy that those American citizens who live closest to the White House and the Capitol have no voting representation in Congress, minimal rights of self-government, minimal control over local revenue, and no control over judicial appointments.

As Rev. Jesse Jackson has noted, DC citizens face all of the obligations of democracy, but reap none of its benefits. We pay more federal income taxes per capita than every state except for Alaska. And our citizens fight and die for their country in wars.

DC citizens also pay disproportionately high local taxes because the federal government prohibits income taxes from being imposed on people who commute to work in the District but live in other states. This amounts to 60 percent of the city's workforce and costs DC $1.2 billion annually. The federal government also prohibits the imposition of property taxes on federal land and sales taxes on items sold there—exempting approximately 50 percent of all real estate and 50 percent of all sales from taxation, according to Jackson. The federal government's annual payment to the District has never matched the revenue lost by these despotic restrictions, and only accounts for approximately 13 percent of the city budget—87 percent comes from local taxes.

Just as odious is the intervention of George Bush and Congress in the right of DC citizens to make their own laws. They routinely overturn locally passed laws allowing the use of local tax revenues to give poor women full reproductive rights. They attempt to block locally passed gun control provisions. They regularly hold the city's budget hostage on behalf of their own parochial and venal interests.

DC citizens voted overwhelmingly to become a state. So why has their wish been denied? Cut through all the malarkey put forward by right-wing Republicans about the problems of DC government and the intent of the Constitution and every other asinine argument they dream up. It all comes down to one thing: race. If most DC citizens were white, New Columbia would be America's 51st state today. Forget about democracy. If there is one principle Bush and his cronies stand for, it's keeping the Senate from getting two new liberal, Democratic, African American members, especially when one is likely to be Jackson.

Oh, I forgot Bush's other principle—not paying state income taxes. He keeps his Houston hotel room (Texas doesn't have an income tax) to avoid paying them in Maine; but if DC became a state, poor George might have to pay some hefty taxes in the city that's been his real home for the past two decades.

SENATOR JESSE JACKSON?
BY BRADLEY O'LEARY

Don't expect to see Jesse Jackson campaign for Bill Clinton until October 10th, but from that date on, Jackson will be tireless in his efforts to elect Bill Clinton president, because he's got the best deal he could possibly expect out of this year's election.

Elect Clinton president, and Jackson can expect a DC statehood bill passed by Congress. The Democrats plan to tie it to a Puerto Rican statehood bill, and leave it up to the citizens of Puerto Rico to turn down statehood.

DC statehood is already supported by Ron Brown, chairman of the Democratic Party, and publicly or privately supported by 95 percent of the Democratic members of the U.S. Senate and House of Representatives and most Democratic governors.

The bill, surely to be signed into law if Clinton is elected president, would give big government two additional U.S. senators with full voting rights, who would constantly vote to expand federal powers, increase taxes, and develop more welfare programs.

If the DNC, Bill Clinton, and Jesse Jackson's plan to

grant statehood to DC was to succeed, just what kind of legislation would these senators likely propose? We can get a taste of this by laws passed or contemplated by the DC City Council.

- Allow criminals to be released on bail by the signature of a friend
- Oppose capital punishment
- Allow unmarried adults who live together to register as "domestic partners" no matter their sexual orientation
- Make "domestic partners" eligible for health insurance benefits the same as married couples
- Prohibit insurance companies from testing applicants for the AIDS virus
- Ban ownership and possession of any handgun, rifle or shotgun
- Substantially increase the minimum wage
- Increase the unemployment compensation rate
- Increase welfare programs
- Allow unrestricted abortion rights—free from parental consent
- Support birth-to-grave social welfare system of socialized medicine and free national health care with no opportunity to choose your own doctor
- Distribute condoms in high schools
- Distribute free needles to addicts
- Provide federally funded drug-rehab on demand
- Force all privately owned businesses with fifteen or more employees to give preference to minority-owned business bids/contracts
- From the "state" with the least effective, but second most expensive education system in the nation, impose an education plan that prohibits discipline in schools

Don't be fooled by Democratic "spin doctors" who tell you this legislation could never happen without the votes of thirty-eight states. The Jesse Jackson Rainbow Coalition's own literature admits that a simple majority vote in both houses of the U.S. Congress and the president's signature is all that is needed.

So is it any wonder that all Bill Clinton has to do to have Jesse Jackson's full cooperation and mobilization of his supporters is to refer to him as Senator Jesse Jackson? Clinton is ready to pay that price, but is America?

15 / Personalities

Whether you are a conservative or a liberal will go a long way in determining how you feel about the prominent political figures of our time. Does Ronald Reagan make your knees weak? Or do you think he was a better movie actor than a president? How about Bill Clinton—do you love him or loathe him? Did George Bush get a bum rap? Or was he as bad a president as Clinton said he was?

Our different takes on the character issue during the 1992 presidential campaign illustrate how liberals felt about George Bush and how conservatives saw Bill Clinton.

TRUST (OCTOBER 1992)

WHOM DO YOU TRUST?
BY BRADLEY O'LEARY

Although the principal issue that will decide this election will not be the issue of trust, it is a fair issue for Americans to think about when Americans choose a president.

Many Americans disagreed with U.S. involvement in Vietnam. We have been going through a healing process the last few years, with each side moving toward reconciliation—not just with each other, but also with the Soviet Union, Vietnam, and our enemies of the past. We have not asked in recent years for people to feel ashamed of how they felt or where they stood.

My problem with Bill Clinton is that he shows no pride in what his beliefs were, and at every step in his political career, by hiding his actions, he is really telling us he is ashamed of them.

In 1978, when he ran for governor of Arkansas, Clinton publicly denied that he had an ROTC deferment. In 1982, during his third run for governor, Clinton denied ever being opposed to the draft. Today in his run for the presidency, I'm as confused by the charges as I am by his answers.

But, I know this: there are a lot of politicians and others that I've heard of who used every means they could think of to secure a place in the reserves or in an ROTC program, but he is the only politician I've heard of who, having secured that coveted prize, turned his back on it.

Early in his campaign, there were published reports about how Clinton helped a loyal campaign worker secure a patronage job. A worker who went on to become his friend, someone with whom he felt comfortable calling to discuss his private thoughts and even his dreams and aspirations. When this person became a political liability for him, Clinton once again felt a sense of shame at his earlier actions and denied that their friendship was anything more that the most casual of relationships.

And, when Clinton was elected governor of Arkansas, he did so after promising to protect the rights of Arkansas' hunters and gun owners. Clinton's administration doubled the tax on hunters and twice Clinton vetoed legislation that would have prevented New York City- or Washington, DC-style gun laws from being enacted in Arkansas. Such legislation has already been enacted in forty-one other states, but because of Clinton, not in the state where Clinton vowed to protect the rights of hunters and law-abiding gun owners.

In the early years when he was running for president, Clinton headed up the conservative Democratic Leadership Council (DLC), an organization often at odds with the more liberal members of the Democratic Party. But, when he ran in the Democratic primaries, Clinton put aside the philosophy of the DLC and espoused a more liberal ideology that would be popular with Democratic primary voters. Today, Clinton is dealing with an electorate that is more moderate and he now portrays himself as a moderate.

If he is elected president, Clinton will be elected with a very liberal spend and tax Democratic Congress. Can you really trust him to be the same man you voted for? Or will he be the same man he's always been: a political chameleon ready to do or say whatever it takes to win.

I'm not altogether sure if "trust" can be clearly understood by most voters unless we ask the question in two meaningful ways:

First: If Clinton had been president when the conflict with Saddam Hussein had come about, would he have ignored the unanimous opinion of the Democratic leadership in the Senate and House and even the opposition of most of his Cabinet members, including his probable secretary of defense, to kick Saddam Hussein out of Kuwait?

Second: With the Democratic leadership in Congress committed to their party platform's call for increased spending on social programs of approximately $500 billion (this includes their health care proposals), would Clinton deny them these programs or would he go along with Democratic congressional proposals to raise taxes on everyone who earns $30,000 a year or more?

Whom do you trust?

WOULD YOU BUY A USED CAR FROM BUSH?
BY VICTOR KAMBER

For George Bush to attack Bill Clinton as "untrustworthy" is a little like Richard Nixon having the gall to accuse an opponent of being a crook. It's an issue that is ricocheting back and smashing Bush right in the face.

Let's look at the record:

- **1988:** George Bush proclaims "Read my lips: no new taxes!"
- **1990:** George Bush signs into law a massive package of tax increases.
- **September 9, 1992:** George Bush says he won't raise taxes again, "Never, ever!"
- **September 10, 1992:** White House spokesman Marlin Fitzwater says Bush's statement of the previous day "wasn't a pledge, no."

Trust George Bush? The man has spent his political career talking out of both sides of his mouth. Even worse, his words have no bearing on his actions.

Let's look again at the record.

- **The Economy:** In 1988, Bush promised to create 30 million jobs over the next 8 years. At the rate he has been moving, it will take Bush more than 100 years to fulfill his promise.
- **The Environment:** In 1988, George Bush proclaimed he will be the "environmental president." But then he assigned Dan Quayle authority, through the "Competitiveness Council," to undo virtually every major environmental regulation on the book. He singlehandedly sabotaged the creation of a worldwide strategy to stop global

warming in Rio de Janeiro. And he demagogued the spotted owl issue in an attempt to undermine the Endangered Species Act.

- **Education:** Bush also said he would be the "education president." Yet today more than two out of every three children who are eligible for Head Start cannot participate. Over 4 million disadvantaged children are denied reading and math assistance. Literacy programs serve only 1 in 20 adults who need help. And the nation's education budget is two-thirds what it was in 1980 before Reagan and Bush took office.

- **Iran-Contra:** When Bush told the world he was "out of the loop" on the decision to trade arms for hostages, Defense Secretary Casper Weinberger called Secretary of State George Schultz to express his outrage at Bush's lie. And a former National Security Council official made clear that he kept Bush well informed about what transpired. Despite incontrovertible evidence that Bush not only knew, but even approved of, what was going on, he refuses to give the American people any explanation of his actions.

- **Family Values:** After satiating the GOP's loony right wing at the 1992 Republican Convention by trumpeting himself as the guardian of "family values," Bush vetoed the number one pro-family bill sent to his desk, the Family and Medical Leave Act. Now anyone who loses a job because he or she needs time off to care for a newborn baby or ill relative knows whom to blame: "Mr. Family Values," George Bush.

- **Abortion:** Before running for president in 1980, Bush was a supporter of Planned Parenthood and generally had a pro-choice position. Since then, he has taken the most extreme anti-abortion stance possible, even imposing an outrageous "gag rule," prohibiting federally funded clinics from discussing the option of abortion with patients.

The bottom line is George Bush can't be trusted on anything because he stands for nothing except staying in power. As Bush himself said, he will do anything to get re-elected. Based on the above evidence, it's clear that pledge includes lying to the American people.

Would you buy a used car from this man?

• • •

Very few political figures excite such loyalty and such hostility as First Lady Hillary Rodham Clinton. Liberals love her—she's the very model of a tough, smart career woman, who is also a caring individual devoted to her family. Conservatives see her as an abrasive, ambitious, and possibly dishonest shyster lawyer. Here's how we feel about the First Lady.

HILLARY CLINTON (MAY 1993)

A STRONG WOMAN
BY VICTOR KAMBER

> *The world is full of weak men that have always been scared of strong women, and I say, to heck with them—let 'em go and wallow in their own insecurities.*

With those typically blunt words (spoken on ABC News's *Nightline*), consultant James Carville pointedly summarized the essence of the right wing's extraordinary hostility toward Hillary Rodham Clinton.

Let's face it. Here is a woman who is one of the nation's top 100 lawyers, a successful attorney who has used her exceptional skills to advance the well-being of the nation's forgotten population—our children. If she wasn't married to Bill Clinton, she would have been at the top of any credible list for attorney general or secretary of health and human services.

Right wingers just can't handle the fact that a brilliant, independent career woman is married to the president of the United States. The sheer viciousness, vehemence, and malevolence of their reaction toward her—matched only by their response to gays in the military—strongly suggests they find both a threat to their ever-so-fragile masculinity.

The fact is that Hillary Rodham Clinton is as qualified as anyone in the country to craft a comprehensive national health care reform package that will control costs, preserve quality, and insure all Americans. After all, Bill Clinton's entire presidency is riding on this issue (along with the economy). He could only afford to make this appointment based on one criterion—ability—and that is what he did.

The right wing attacks Hillary Rodham Clinton ostensibly for her political views, complaining that she has an "ultra-liberal" hidden agenda. Get real. While committed to economic and social justice, she is as pragmatic as they come, and as old-fashioned and sexist as it may sound, her first priority is advancing her husband's career.

The fact that her work as the former chair of the Children's Defense Fund is often cited makes this accusation all the more ludicrous. If fighting poverty and child abuse and advocating programs such as Head Start, WIC (assistance to women, infants and children), and better child care makes one an "ultra-liberal," then any red-blooded American should be proud to carry that label.

If further evidence of her lack of a "hidden agenda" is needed, then look at her work chairing then-Governor Clinton's Arkansas education reform commission. She didn't hesitate to recommend many controversial proposals, some of which went against liberal orthodoxy and initially alienated key Democratic constituencies, such as the teachers' unions. Ultimately, the education reform package that she developed became the high point of her husband's governorship.

As far as I'm concerned, I want Hillary Rodham Clinton's stamp on every single aspect of the Clinton presidency. The more she makes her mark, the more successful he will be. And the more the right wing figuratively grabs its collective crotch and squeals, the more we'll know that she's doing the right thing.

WHO ELECTED HER?
BY BRADLEY O'LEARY

Even though Hillary Clinton seems to be on a first name basis with Eleanor Roosevelt from imaginary conversations they've had, she's no reincarnation of Eleanor Roosevelt. At best she may be described as a Clinton's Lady Macbeth. From an activist standpoint she fits the role model of Winnie Mandela. We might even consider her to be the kindly-looking woodcutter Geppetto who created Pinnochio and always pulled his strings.

During the Reagan years, a person's success was judged on a certain set of standards that Hillary and Bill Clinton said were all wrong. What's more, all those left-wing kooks who are now in the White House agreed that those standards were wrong. By Democratic Party standards, a lawyer who served on foreign multi-national corporate boards and American corporate boards, and made over $120,000 serving on those boards was greedy. A lawyer who served on a corporate board of one of the richest men in America was greedy. A lawyer who was smart enough to invest in a South African corporation that is notorious for underpaying black labor and making a profit from it was greedy. A lawyer who understood the stock market, placing calls and puts, and playing "short," and made money out of it was greedy. Calling this person successful wasn't enough according to Democrats. That shouldn't have been a measure of success they claimed. That sort of "success" was nothing more than greed. Well folks, I've just described Hillary Clinton. She serves on boards. She's made lots of money. She's sold stocks short for profit. And that's the reason a number of the legal fraternity consider her successful.

The Clintons also came to Washington promising a better ethics standard in government. Now that they're in Washington they've shown that their ethical standards are substantially lower than those of Ronald Reagan or George Bush. Hillary's "stealth" task force meetings demonstrate that she and her husband are not in favor of open government. It took a court decision to finally require that the First Lady comply with the law by opening her task force meetings to the public. Believe me my friends, this is not the first time that Hillary has ignored government ethics. As chairman of the Legal Services Committee she allowed the use of $300 million of your taxes to run left-wing federal government-sponsored programs that most people considered to be rife with illegality. She repeatedly ignored ethics laws. She paid to fund activists to help them defeat California's Proposition 9, which would have cut taxes in half. She also paid activists to combat programs launched by Ronald Reagan. She finally had to be kicked off the board by the courts. This latest closed-government stealth attempt by her will turn the nation's health care system—which provides first-rate quality care at an 85 percent nationally insured rate—into a system that will insure 100 percent of the people who will have access to a third-rate medical system. She saw no reason to eliminate herself from representing a client before her husband's Arkansas Securities Commission—a client who was in big trouble with the government. Her ethical standards are so low that no less a "paragon of virtue" than the U.S. House of Representatives felt that she had to be opposed in her "stealth" task force efforts.

As an activist she's about as left-wing as they come. She helped to funnel $5,000 to fund a left-wing group supporting the Sandinistas; $20,000 to the hard-left wacko Christic Institute; $15,000 to the National Lawyers Group, an organization with close ties to the American Communist Party; and money for William Kunstler's Chicago Seven, a left-wing lawyer center for constitutional study.

In college she was associate editor of a publication that showed drawings depicting the police as pigs. Is it any wonder she was totally silent when the rap singer Ice T called on his audience to kill cops? I guess her disdain for people in uniform isn't only restricted to members of the military. She is in favor of granting to children the same procedural rights granted to adults. In other words, she wants to be able to create jobs for her buddies in the legal profession so kids can hire them to settle family disputes—a move that would allow the government, through the court system, to run your family. She also supports a tax system that would require hunters and sportsmen to pay a health care tax whenever they wanted to buy ammunition.

When you get down to it, here is a woman who has now given up what under Ronald Reagan and George Bush guidelines would be called a successful career. And now she wants to use her husband's influence, power, and position to get "invitations" to get money, to get power and to get influence. I'm glad she married well. You'll never see Hillary Clinton giving Bill Clinton those adoring looks like Nancy Reagan gave to Ronald Reagan. I think that's why Al Gore was probably selected as Vice President, so he could do that. After all, Hillary Clinton has more senior advisors than Al Gore does. I guess we know what roles Al Gore and Hillary Clinton play.

This woman has been described by staff people as destructive and manipulative. She's been able to stop senior members of the Democratic Leadership Council from getting any kind of job in the Clinton administration. You had better believe that she and Susan Thomases are the ones who actively campaigned against these people getting jobs.

My thoughts are best summed up by the bumper sticker I saw the other day that read: "Who elected HER?"

16 / Bonus Quiz

Now that you've read our book, you should know where you stand. But you might find the need for further investigation. Now that you've read our liberal and conservative arguments, have we changed your mind on any of the issues? Have we brought you closer to one side or the other? And if you scored liberal on one and conservative on another, here's a chance to break the tie.

This bonus quiz has many different uses. But most of all it's meant to be fun and provide the basis for stimulating discussions (we won't call them arguments) at home, school or office.

1. **If you had an opportunity to attend a concert, which of the following would you go to:**

   ☐ Frank Sinatra or
   ☐ Bruce Springsteen
   _____
   ☐ Barbara Mandrell or
   ☐ Barbra Streisand

2. **Do you believe that teachers should have the right to spank children?**

   ☐ Yes
   ☐ No

3. **If you have an opportunity to receive a free car of equal value as a gift, which would you choose:**

   ☐ A Volvo
   ☐ An Oldsmobile

4. **If you had an opportunity to vote for one of the following people for President of the United States, who would you vote for:**

   ☐ Richard Nixon
   ☐ Lyndon Johnson

5. **Whose political views do you consider to be more extreme?**

   ☐ Pat Buchanan
   ☐ Jesse Jackson

6. **Which of the following child and family experts has views closer to your views in raising children?**

   ☐ Dr. T. Berry Brazelton
   ☐ Dr. James Dobson

7. **If there were only two television channels, which one would you watch?**

   ☐ MTV
   ☐ The Nashville Network

8. **If there were only two television shows on, which one would you watch:**

   ☐ Rush Limbaugh
   ☐ Phil Donahue

9. **If you were going to buy insurance from one of the following two people, who would you feel more comfortable buying it from?**

   ☐ Nancy Reagan
   ☐ Hillary Rodham Clinton

10. **Of the following two movies, which one more closely reflects your view of American history from the 1960s and 1970s?**

    ☐ *Forrest Gump*
    ☐ Oliver Stone's *Nixon*

11. **If you could choose someone to address a senior high school class, whom would you choose:**

    ☐ Dr. Ruth or
    ☐ Pat Robertson
    _____

    ☐ Jesse Helms or
    ☐ Ted Kennedy

12. **Do you believe in mandatory drug testing for the following people: (check all that apply.)**

    ☐ Welfare recipients
    ☐ College aid recipients
    ☐ Driver's license applicants
    ☐ Applicants for U.S. citizenship

13. **Who would you rather have lunch with:**

    ☐ Al Gore
    ☐ Dan Quayle

14. **Do you believe that the federal government or state governments are better able to administer key programs such as welfare?**

    ☐ Federal
    ☐ State

15. **Do you believe that when people buy a handgun:**

    ☐ They should have to wait five days to have their records checked
    ☐ They should have their records checked instantly on a computer

16. Should federal judges have term limits?

☐ Yes
☐ No

17. ☐ Do you support a cut in the capital gains tax because it will spur new job-creating investment

OR

☐ **Do you oppose a cut in the capital gains tax because it will mostly benefit the rich.**

18. Should sex offenders be castrated?

☐ Yes
☐ No

19. Should we raise the minimum wage or keep it the same?

☐ Raise
☐ Keep the same

20. Should animals be used for testing and research?

☐ Yes
☐ No

21. Should prisoners be forced to work on chain gangs?

☐ Yes
☐ No

22. What do you see as the bigger problem facing America?

☐ Too many government regulations on business
or
☐ Too few protections from corporate abuses

☐ Not enough money spent on the root causes of crime or
☐ Lack of prison space and too many plea bargains

☐ Obstacles to unions organizing workers so they can negotiate higher wages and benefits or
☐ Obstacles to businesses making themselves more globally competitive

☐ Welfare recipients refusing to work because they have no work ethic or
☐ Welfare recipients unable to work because of the lack of jobs and child care

☐ Frivolous lawsuits and excessive jury awards against product manufacturers or
☐ Consumers' health and safety put at risk by faulty products

SCORING

Give yourself 1 point for each conservative answer and 0 points for each liberal answer. Again, this is not a value judgment on liberals or conservatives, it is just a way of measuring your stand on the issue.

1. Sinatra = 1   Springsteen = 0
    Mandrell = 1   Streisand = 0
2. Yes = 1   No = 0
3. Volvo = 0   Oldsmobile = 1
4. Nixon = 1   Johnson = 0
5. Buchanan = 0   Jackson = 1
6. Brazelton = 0   Dobson = 1
7. MTV = 0   The Nashville Network = 1
8. Rush Limbaugh = 1   Phil Donahue = 0
9. Nancy Reagan = 1   Hillary Rodham Clinton = 0
10. *Forrest Gump* = 1   *Nixon* = 0
11. Dr. Ruth = 0   Pat Robertson = 1
    Jesse Helms = 1   Ted Kennedy = 0

12. Give yourself 1 point for each checked (maximum of 4).
13. Al Gore = 0 Dan Quayle = 1
14. Federal = 0 State = 1
15. 5 days = 0 Instantly = 1
16. Yes = 1 No = 0
17. Support cut = 1 Oppose cut = 0
18. Yes = 1 No = 0
19. Raise = 0 Keep the same = 1
20. Yes = 1 No = 0
21. Yes = 1 No = 0
22. Too many = 1 Too few = 0
    Not enough = 0 Lack of prison space = 1
    Obstacles to unions = 0 Obstacles to businesses = 1
    Refusing to work = 1 Unable to work = 0
    Frivilous lawsuits = 1 Consumers' health = 0

Score Range (with our estimate of where several prominent celebrities might stand on the political spectrum):

0–3	100 percent liberal (Paul Newman)
4–7	Very liberal (Barbra Streisand)
8–11	Liberal (Tom Hanks)
12–15	Moderate to Liberal (David Letterman)
16–19	Moderate to Conservative (Jay Leno)
20–23	Conservative (Tom Selleck)
24–27	Very conservative (Charlton Heston)
28–31	100 percent conservative (Mel Gibson)

We hope that you have enjoyed reading this book and that we have helped you to answer the questions of whether you are a conservative or a liberal and where you stand on the issues.

We also hope that we have provoked further questions and a lively debate.

Please drop us a note and let us know how you did on the quizzes or if you have any suggestions for future quizzes.

Boru Publishing
12004-B Commonwealth Way
Austin, TX 78759

Thank you.

* * * *

If you would like to listen to the *O'Leary/Kamber Radio Report*, please contact your local NBC Network radio station for air times. The show is a one-hour, weekly point-counterpoint on one of the important issues facing America that week.

Ordering Information

To order the books published by Brad O'Leary or Vic Kamber at wholesale prices for bookstores, contact the **National Book Network**, 4720 Boston Way, Lanham, Maryland 20706. Telephone: (800) 462-6420.

To order individual books, please call 1-800-847-4800.